FOOD FOR THE JOURNEY

Theological Foundations of the Catholic Healthcare Ministry

JULIANA CASEY, IHM

THE CATHOLIC HEALTH ASSOCIATION
OF THE UNITED STATES
ST. LOUIS

Copyright 1991
by
The Catholic Health Association of the United States
4455 Woodson Road
St. Louis, MO 63134-3797

ISBN 0-87125-194-9

*The Bible text is from the Revised Standard Version Bible, copyright 1946, 1952, 1971
by the Division of Christian Education of the National Council of Churches of Christ in
the USA, and used by permission.

CONTENTS

FOREWORD

F ive years ago, when I was invited to become a bishop-member of the
Catholic Health Association Board of Trustees, I demurred on the grounds
that I knew very little about Catholic healthcare as a ministry and nothing at all
about the bewildering demands of Catholic hospital administration. When it
was gently suggested that it might be about time to remedy that ignorance, I
reluctantly accepted and thereby began one of the great learning experiences
of my life in the Church. I soon found that I was not alone in my inability to
identify the elements of Catholic healthcare. That ministry, so long associated
with the corneted Daughters of Charity of St. Vincent De Paul on the
battlefield or during the plague, has become so institutionalized in our own
era that many are unable to distinguish what is specifically Catholic about, for
example, an 1,100-bed hospital operated by a Catholic healthcare system as
opposed to a public hospital or one managed by a for-profit enterprise. In this
decade when the healthcare ministry is challenged on many fronts there is a
greater need than ever to focus on the Catholic identity of our institutions. In
face of that need, the CHA board authorized a study that would bring fresh
articulation to these matters. Contributors to the process brought wide-
ranging suggestions about approaches to be taken to provide for theological
accuracy and contemporary idiom. A multi-phased approach was devised, of
which the present volume is the happy and brilliant conclusion.

In the work before us, Sr. Juliana Casey, IHM, brings into one coherent
statement many reflections on abstract truth and complex experience. It is a
work that flows smoothly not only because of its easy style but because its
theological content is grounded in the Christian's experience of life and death,
of peace, comfort and healing. Christ himself is the ultimate expression of
God's compassion, and in the stories of the Gospel we are made to see the
divine pity at work in his healing touch. In his redemptive sacrifice Christ
challenges the human family to accept the saving power of God to heal the
wounds of sin and self-destruction. From its inception the Church, driven by
the dynamic power of the Spirit, has provided these same manifestations of
God's healing love, present to us in moments of conflict, illness, and death.
Today as much as ever Catholic healthcare is a revelation of this mystery. Sr.
Juliana's work spells this out for us in admirable fashion as she tells the story
of Catholic healthcare as a sacrament of Christ's healing mercy in our day. As
healing was an essential part of Christ's revelation, so it must continue to be a
part of the Church's life.

I cannot conclude this brief introduction without expressing deepest gratitude to the religious congregations who almost alone and at great cost have preserved the healthcare ministry in the Church. The continuation of this mission will doubtless see many new forms of sponsorship in the years ahead, but these religious—and the dioceses who joined them—had so sharp and compelling an understanding of Christ's healing ministry that the Church's healthcare institutions and ministry will surely continue the great and glorious work of manifesting God's love and mercy in our midst.

Most Rev. Thomas C. Kelly, OP
Archbishop of Louisville
Member, CHA board of trustees

PREFACE

If Catholic healthcare is to continue as a vital and important ministry within the Church, its leaders must understand its significance and be committed to its continuance. For this to happen, leaders in Catholic healthcare must be provided with resources that both deepen undestanding and enhance commitment. The Catholic Health Association of the United States (CHA) has taken an active role in the creation and provision of such resources.

In 1987, CHA published *The Dynamics of Catholic Identity in Healthcare*. This work was intended to be "... the initial step in CHA's concerted effort to formulate a clear understanding of the theology and practical implications of Catholic identity."[1] It approached the question of Catholic identity from the perspective of the Church's sacramental nature and Catholic healthcare's participation in that sacramental nature. In 1988, CHA published its leadership formation document, *Healthcare Leadership: Shaping a Tomorrow*. This document provides an overview of the elements of both organizational and individual leadership development. It describes a core curriculum for those areas of importance to the leader in Catholic healthcare, such as "God and Sacraments," "Gospel Values," and "Collaboration." *Healthcare Leadership* flows from the Catholic identity document. The understanding of Catholic healthcare, which is at the heart of the formation document, is that of the sacramentality of the healthcare ministry. "*Catholic* healthcare ministry, therefore, is *sacramental* ministry. This ministry is more than business, more than efficiency, more than 'bottom-line' calculations. It is participation in and continuation of a sacred, holy, and healing presence among all people."[2]

These two texts have become a foundation on which other work can be built. *Food for the Journey: Theological Foundations of the Catholic Healthcare Ministry* is CHA's most recent contribution to the ongoing effort to articulate the theological grounding of Catholic healthcare. *Food for the Journey*, which also views the healthcare ministry from a sacramental perspective, develops some of the central themes of *Healthcare Leadership*, such as the relationship of the healthcare ministry to the Catholic Church, the mission and ministry of Jesus Christ, the social teaching of the Church, and healthcare of the poor. At other times, *Food for the Journey* moves beyond *Healthcare Leadership* as it examines themes such as suffering and dying in the Judaic-Christian tradition, stewardship, and characteristics of a spirituality for healthcare personnel.

All three texts pay special attention to the leader's experience of healthcare in today's world. Each seeks to bring the light and the wisdom of our faith tradition to bear on that experience. With the publication of *Food for the Journey,* a new and important resource is made available for all those committed to the ministry of Catholic healthcare.

John E. Curley, Jr.
President
The Catholic Health Association
of the United States

---

1. *The Dynamics of Catholic Identity in Healthcare: A Working Document,* Catholic Health Association, St. Louis, 1987, p. v.
2. *Healthcare Leadership: Shaping a Tomorrow,* Catholic Health Association, St. Louis, 1988, p. xiv.

ACKNOWLEDGMENTS

One never writes a book alone. Many people are involved. They are the ones whose wisdom teaches us, whose questions sharpen our insight, and whose skills enhance our own. Many such people have been part of the creation of *Food for the Journey.* The members of CHA's Division of Theology, Mission, and Ethics read versions of the manuscript and provided valuable insights. Rev. Joe Kukura, vice president of the Division, offered many helpful suggestions and constant encouragement. Jeanette McMillin faithfully and skillfully typed many drafts of this work. I am grateful for the insights, the skills, and the encouragement.

I am most grateful, however, to the persons whose dedication to the ministry of healthcare is always a source of inspiration. Some of their stories appear anonymously in this book. The scope of their commitment, however, can never be captured in words. Their wisdom, insight, and skill have been food for my journey, and it is to them that this work is dedicated.

PROLOGUE

FOOD FOR THE JOURNEY

The gospel of Matthew tells us that Jesus called his disciples to him, gave them instructions, and then sent them on a journey. His instructions were to "preach as you go, saying, 'The kingdom of heaven is at hand.' Heal the sick, raise the dead, cleanse lepers, cast out demons" (Mt 10:7). Since that moment, women and men of faith have continued to seek to heal the sick in the belief that to do so was to follow the call of the gospel.

The Catholic Church has always been blessed with those who would journey forth in service to the suffering members of society. Healthcare has always been an important ministry within the Church—a holy work. The journey of the healthcare giver has always been viewed as a blessed journey.

For those on the journey, however, its blessedness is not always obvious. Healthcare is filled with pain and fraught with difficulties. It is often lonely and defeating work. Those who serve in healthcare sometimes forget its holiness in the midst of everyday pressures and stress. Sometimes, the journey seems as one long desert, and one can starve in the desert.

Everyone who journeys needs provisions for the journey, needs food along the way. Healthcare professionals often find nourishment in the wonders their work can achieve, in the generosity and inspiration of their co-workers, and in the appreciation of those they help. For those who serve in Catholic healthcare, there is still another source of nourishment: the riches of Catholic theology.

Theology is often seen as a serious and difficult science. It has its own opaque language, its own specialties, its own discipline. Theology is something some people study and write about in books with copious footnotes in foreign languages. This aspect to theology is an important one. Faith is worthy of serious and difficult study. Opaque language is sometimes the only language in which to express mystery. Footnotes are often a way to continue a conversation. However, that is not all there is to theology. Every believer "does" theology. Each time we try to understand the meaning of our experience in light of what we know of God, faith, and the gospel, we are theologizing. We are allowing the light of revelation to illumine our life. An example will help clarify this idea.

A young man stood at the bedside of his dying father. His father was himself young, and his anguished suffering seemed to make no sense. His son had watched him in pain for a long time. Now he was dying. Tied to the foot of the bed were three or four helium balloons that had been sent by a friend.

1

When his father died, the young man left the room. He returned shortly with a pair of scissors. He looked at his mother, who simply nodded her head and said, "Yes." The young man then cut the ribbons holding the balloons, took them outside, and set them free to sail into the night sky.

This young man's actions speak a profound theology. They tell us that he understands death as a freeing from suffering, as an entrance into a new life. They also tell us that his God is one who ultimately gives life and that death is not the final victor. Our own actions may be less dramatic, our words confused at times, and our questions greater than any answers we can find. Each time we ask questions of faith, however, each time we try to speak meaning in light of God's self-revelation, we are doing theology. When this happens, theology is no longer merely science; it is life. It enriches us, enlivens us, and sustains us on the journey.

This work is an attempt to theologize on the experience of Catholic healthcare. It seeks to explore some basic themes of the Catholic, Judaic-Christian tradition to allow that tradition to illumine our experience. It is not an attempt to write a scholarly treatise on the meaning of Catholic healthcare, and it does not pretend to be exhaustive of either the tradition or the experience. It does not answer any of the specific—and difficult—questions that face Catholic healthcare today. It does suggest avenues, memories, and attitudes that might be useful in answering those questions.

The themes explored are (1) the presence of God in human experience, (2) the mission and ministry of Jesus Christ, (3) the Church and healthcare, (4) the meaning of suffering, (5) the Christian understanding of death, (6) the social teachings of the Church and healthcare of the poor, (7) faithful stewardship, and (8) the moral life and healthcare. The epilogue suggests some characteristics of a spirituality of healthcare. An appendix offers some questions for reflection and discussion. Each theme is approached from the perspective of human experience and in light of the tradition's resources. It is hoped that each provides some food for the journey.

Food given to a traveller often has a mysterious quality. The Israelites were nourished by manna from heaven. Elijah the prophet was fed by ravens. Sometimes sharing food with a traveller can be healing. A widow once found this to be true. In the midst of a famine in the land, she was approached by the prophet Elijah, who asked her for food. She had only a little grain and some oil, she said, and with that she planned to make a last meal for herself and her son, "that we may eat it and die" (2 Kings 17:12). Elijah told her that the grain and oil would not be used up and that she should make him a little cake with it first, then feed her son and herself. Amazingly, she did so, and the grain and the oil were not used up. In fact, they continued to provide food for several days. One day, however, the widow's son became very ill. The widow blamed Elijah, but Elijah brought the son back to life. The widow then turned to this man to whom she had given food and said: "Now I know that you are a man of God, and that the word of the Lord in your mouth is truth" (17:24).

Food shared on a journey often does more than keep us alive. Sometimes it becomes the essence of miracles and of wonder. It is hoped that the food of our faith tradition, when it is shared, will lighten the journey, allow the desert to bloom at times, lead us to recognize the people of God in our midst, and free us to share our own food.

1

"Take Off Your Shoes, This Is Holy Ground"

THE PRESENCE OF GOD IN HUMAN EXPERIENCE

The entrances to healthcare facilities are interesting places. Some are large and beautifully decorated; some are small and very crowded. Entrances reveal much about what occurs in a place, what type of spirit it has. Most of them have pictures or statues that represent the great people connected to the facility. They might be the foundress of the religious congregation, the hospital's first administrator, a group of pioneers who first came to the area, or a particularly visionary person in the facility's history. Sometimes the images are biblical ones: the Good Samaritan, the Works of Mercy, the Mother of God, the Good Shepherd.

Whatever the image, all these pictures and statues are both sign and remembrance. They are sign to all who enter that what happens in this place happens for a reason and in a spirit of faith and caring. They invite all who enter to remember both the vision and the spirit of those who brought the place into existence. They recall the vision, the insight of great men and women. These are the people who heard God's call and saw God's face in suffering people. They are ones who recognized that healthcare is blessed work and holy ministry. They had a "sixth sense," as it were, that enabled them to recognize divine presence in the midst of human experience.

The Judaic-Christian tradition firmly believes that God is present in life. It, too, looks to holy men and women as sign and as remembrance. The lives of two of these, Moses and Jesus, can serve to show us how and why God acts in our lives.

MOSES, EXTRAORDINARY MAN

Moses led an extraordinary life. Son of a slave in Egypt, kept hidden for the first three months of his life, placed in a basket by a river's bank, raised as a son by Pharoah's daughter, slayer of an Egyptian slave master, fugitive in the land of Midian . . . Moses' life was not an ordinary one. Called to free a people, reluctant leader during 40 years of desert wandering, parter of waters, and receiver of God's law, Moses was unique in history. There was "none like him for all the signs and the wonders which the Lord sent him to do in the land of Egypt, to Pharoah and to all his servants and to all his land, and for all the mighty power and all the great and terrible deeds which Moses wrought in the sight of all Israel" (Deut 34:11-12).

What *really* made Moses extraordinary, however, is that he saw and spoke with God. "And there has not arisen a prophet since in Israel like Moses, whom the Lord knew face to face" (Deut 34:10). Despite all the dramatic events of his early years, the great turning point for Moses came in the midst of the ordinary tasks of everyday life. While tending the sheep of his father-in-law, Moses saw an unusual sight and went to investigate. He found himself standing on holy ground, speaking with God. "Take off your shoes, Moses, for God is present here" (Ex 3:1-6). So began the miracle of the Exodus. Moses, in the company of an ever-present God, was to free people and lead them to a promised land.

His was not an easy task. The journey was difficult, the people were stubborn and recalcitrant, and enemies were abundant. What kept Moses going was the constant presence of God. Only if God shared the people's experience could they go on. When the people reached Mount Sinai, God made a covenant with them. They would be God's people and God would be their God. The people and God belonged to each other. As sign of this covenant, God gave Moses a law for the people. When Moses came down from Mount Sinai with the law in his hands, he discovered that the people had deserted God and were worshipping an idol, a golden calf they had made. Moses, in his great anger, destroyed the tablets that contained the law. God, in even greater anger, declared that the people would have to go on alone: "Go up to a land flowing with milk and honey; but I will not go up among you, lest I consume you in the way, for you are a stiff-necked people" (Ex 33:3). Moses, however, would not agree to do this. He told God that if God would not go with the people, the people would not go: "And he (Moses) said to God, 'If your presence will not go with me, do not carry us up from here. For how shall it be known that I have found favor in your sight, I and your people? Is it not in your going with us, so that we are distinct, I and your people, from all other people that are upon the face of the earth?'" (Ex 33:15-16). God relented, and Moses and his people continued on their journey.

Moses' story is the subject of movies and novels; it is dramatic and inspiring. It is also the subject of faith. The events of his life tell us about God and about the presence of God in human experience. Moses' God did not choose to remain aloof from the people and watch from a distance. Moses' God heard the cries of a suffering people and acted to save them. "I have seen the affliction of my people who are in Egypt, and have heard their cry because of their taskmasters; I know their sufferings, and I have come down to deliver them out of the hand of the Egyptians and to bring them up out of that land to a good and broad land, a land flowing with milk and honey . . ." (Ex 3:7-8).

The God of the Exodus is revealed to us as one deeply immersed in human life, powerfully engaged in a people's suffering, determined to know and be known by human beings. This is a God who *goes with* the people, who calls, cajoles, and commands a people to freedom, to recognition, and to worship. The God of the Exodus, Moses' God, is also the God revealed to us in Jesus Christ.

JESUS, THE INCARNATION OF GOD

The gospel of Matthew tells of a troubled Joseph who does not understand what has happened to his betrothed. When she is found to be pregnant, he decides to divorce her quietly. Then he has a dream, however, and in the dream he is told that the child carried by Mary is to be the people's savior. The gospel then tells us that Jesus' birth is the fulfillment of a great promise given by the prophet Isaiah: "Behold, a maiden shall conceive and bear a son, and his name shall be called Emmanuel" (Is 7:14). Emmanuel means "God with us" (Mt 1:23).

The birth of Jesus, Emmanuel, reveals the depth of union God seeks with humankind. In Jesus, God has entered into the fullness of human experience and has transformed it. All life is now holy ground; all existence is a potential call to "take off our shoes." Moses was the great leader of his people; he was revered in the history of Israel as the greatest of prophets, the one who saw God face to face. His people eventually listened to him because they believed that he knew God. Their own encounters with the divine were mediated by Moses' experience. For his followers, Jesus was the great hope for the salvation of Israel. "But we had hoped that he was the one to redeem Israel" (Lk 24:21). They followed him and listened to his word because they sensed that in meeting him they were meeting God. To touch Jesus was to touch the power of God; to hear his word was to know forgiveness and blessing. Jesus spoke with authority, more authority than that of the prophets.

Jesus said, "Your sins are forgiven," and a man's sins were forgiven. He said, "Arise and walk," and a man rose and walked. Jesus cried, "You are healed," and people were made whole. Jesus spoke and acted with the power of God. This power, the saving action of God, is no longer to be found in a pillar of fire or atop a flaming mountain. It is, rather, in the midst of human life. Jesus' life and teaching show us that the holy is to be found in the ordinary.

One of the most striking characteristics of Jesus' life was its immersion in the normal, the ordinary of his time. He told stories about common tasks such as cleaning a house, planting a crop, going fishing, and hosting a dinner party. He used wild flowers and local birds and landlords and tenants as examples. His friends and companions were people one would meet on the street, in the market, on a fishing boat, at friends' houses, and at the local place of worship. Through him, the divine visited the homes, the workplaces, the relationships, the questions, and the hopes of all men and women.

In Jesus, however, the divine did not merely visit the human reality; it transformed its every aspect. Jesus revealed God's saving activity at work in our world. He showed us that such ordinary events as housecleaning and planting can lead to discovery of grace and call to conversion. A woman cleans her whole house to find a lost coin. She finds it and throws a party in celebration. The party undoubtedly cost her more than the coin she found, but such is the joy of discovering God's presence. A single seed planted in the right soil yields an enormous harvest, more than would ever be expected ... but such things happen when God acts to save.

Jesus' words and actions remind us that salvation comes to those who need it, not necessarily those whom the world deems worthy of it. Tax collectors and sinners are welcomed to his table; a woman who disrupts a dinner party to pay him homage is condemned by others, but blessed by Jesus.

I worked in a hospital in the Appalachian Mountains. I was the business administrator. There was a woman in the hospital who was very sick and running up a huge bill. Her common-law husband, Mr. Slacks, who was always a little tipsy, would come in now and then and put a little something down on the bill. I mean a *little* something—maybe two or three dollars.

One day I was in town with another sister. We had to go to the bank. I saw Mr. Slacks across the street on unsteady legs. I waved. He waved back. The sister I was with said that she wouldn't go into town with me again because I knew all the bums.

The next day I was behind the window at the cashier's office and, lo and behold, who should show up?

"You waved at me yesterday," Mr. Slacks said, and put down two dollars toward the bill. "I like you," he said.

This is where I made my mistake. I said, "I like you, too, Mr. Slacks."

Then he leaned as close to the cashier's window as he could and said, "Tell you what. I got two days off. What do you say you and I go out and get married."

That man came every month for a couple of years and gave us a little bit. I think it was because we recognized who he was.[1]

"... because I knew all the bums." A woman recognizes a person's dignity; she senses worth and perhaps mystery. She reveals God's compassion for those whom the world deems undesirable. She transforms a town's street into holy ground.

CONTINUING PRESENCE, GIFT OF GRACE

Jesus Christ, about whom Joseph had a dream, for whom creation longed, revealed—and was—the presence of God in our midst. Jesus' disciples and friends suspected this and eventually came to believe it. It took them awhile to figure out that Jesus was more than a prophet, more than a miracle worker, more than a great teacher, more than a failed reformer. One can hardly blame them for their slowness. After all, Jesus did not act as the expected Messiah. He did not call for political revolution and did not restore people to long lost thrones. He did not seek power and positions of authority for himself. In fact, the community remembered him as one who said he came to be a servant. Nonetheless, they wanted to be around him, and they found nourishment in his presence. When he was crucified, they were destroyed. When he was raised from the dead, they had difficulty believing it. Sometimes good news is too good to be true.

Jesus' followers slowly came to recognize what God had done through him. They also recognized that his presence continued to be with them. The first Christians underwent a powerful experience that we call Pentecost. They were gifted with God's Spirit, the powerful, gracious, continuing presence of God among them. Transformed by this experience, they were able to proclaim the good news and to continue the work of Jesus. They knew in their own lives the truth of the final words of Matthew's gospel: "I am with you always, to the close of the age" (Mt 28:20).

Fundamental to the Christian tradition is the belief that God's presence continues to be with us in the constant activity of the Spirit and in the life of grace. The God of Moses and Jesus Christ continues to be involved in human life, continues to transform human existence. In the relationship that is grace, God gives self and human beings respond.

Grace signifies the presence of God in the world and in human beings. When God chooses to be present, the sick are made well, the fallen are raised up, the sinners are made just, the dead come back to life, the oppressed experience freedom, and the despairing feel consolation and warm intimacy.

Grace also signifies the openness of human beings to God. It is the ability of human beings to relate to the Infinite, to enter upon a dialogue that wins them their humanity day by day. ...

Grace is always an encounter between a God who gives himself and a human being who does likewise. By its very nature grace is the breaking down of realms or worlds that are closed in upon themselves. Grace is relationship, exodus, communion, encounter, openness, and dialogue. It is the history of two freedoms, the meeting of two loves.[2]

The encounter, the dialogue, the relationship that is grace takes place in our everyday lives. Because of the gift of grace, attentive and receptive persons are able to recognize the presence and the movement of the divine in human experience. All life, therefore, is "holy ground"; all experience has the potential to reveal.

GRACE AND HUMAN EXPERIENCE

Sometimes our experiences speak loudly of God. The beauty of creation, the miracle of birth, and the tenderness of a friend all remind us of a loving Creator. They prompt us to echo the words of the poet: "The world is charged with the grandeur of God. It will flame out, like shining from shook foil."[3] At other times, the movements of our hearts—a great joy, a profound sorrow, an intense longing—turn us toward the One who knows and understands. Most of the time, however, grace speaks softly and can go unheard amidst the noise of our lives. How can we better recognize God's presence in our experience? What does this mean for persons in the healthcare ministry?

The gospels tell us that special things happen when God is recognized in people's lives. A call to conversion is issued and heard. People care about each other, and community is formed. Hope grows.

CONVERSION

Both Matthew and Mark tell us that Jesus' first words to the people were "Repent and believe" (Mk 1:14-15; Mt 4:12-17). His announcement of the kingdom of God is accompanied by a call to conversion. The scriptural term for conversion, *metanoia,* means "to turn," to turn away and to turn toward. The women and men who witnessed Jesus' arrival and who listened to his teaching heard themselves called to turn from their preconceived notions about salvation, about God, and about each other. They were also called to turn toward a God whose mercy was beyond their fondest dreams and to turn toward each other with new compassion and commitment. A vivid description of conversion is given to us in the parable of The Prodigal Son (Lk 15:11-24).

The parable tells the story of two sons and a father. It evokes many well-known and universal themes: the relationship between two sons, the beloved yet profligate youngest child, repentance and forgiveness, and the merciful parent. In the parable, we meet a youngest child who asks for his inheritance, is given it, and then wastes it. He ends up in a foreign land, living as a servant among strangers and non-believers.[4] In total misery, the young man realizes his foolishness, repents, and decides to return to his father. He does not seek to be restored to his position as a son in the household (he lost that right when he took his inheritance and left) but asks only that he be allowed to live as a servant. He turns from his life in exile and turns toward his home. His conversion is a return. As he approaches his home, his father sees him and runs to embrace him. Before he even has a chance to ask forgiveness, the father welcomes him, clothes him in honor, and throws a great party.

The basic pattern of conversion is clear in this case: a sinner, alienated from family, home, and faith, recognizes his misery and returns to find blessing in the embrace of the one who loves him. This pattern would have been familiar, even expected, to those who heard Jesus' parable.

There is another act in the story, however, and another model of conversion. The elder brother comes in from the fields where he had been working and finds a party in progress. He asks a servant what is going on, and when he finds out that the party is in honor of his returned brother, he refuses to join in the celebration. When his father comes out to talk to him, the son berates the father because, despite the son's faithfulness, the father has never done anything so wonderful for him. The father replies that he and the son are always together and that everything the father has is the elder son's. The parable does not tell us if the elder son ever joined the party.

The elder son in the parable has done everything a good son should do. He has not asked for his inheritance, has remained with his father, and has worked hard all the years that the younger son was away. He is the faithful one, the "good" son, but he also must change. If he would join the party, he must accept his father's words and actions. Although the father goes overboard in his welcome of the younger son, the "good" son needs to recognize that the other son also is the inheritor of his father's estate and of his love. The one who is faithful and hard working cannot limit the goodness of another and cannot determine who is worthy of mercy. This son must turn from his previous notions of who should be welcomed and turn toward unbounded forgiveness and celebration.

This second model of conversion would undoubtedly have been more difficult for Jesus' hearers to accept, particularly if they identified with the elder son. The story tells us that whenever God is present, everyone is called to conversion; everyone is invited to mercy and to new understandings of who God is.

The provision of healthcare within a context of faith always calls us to conversion. Sometimes the conversion leads us to recognize our own values and commitment.

> I came to work here because I admired the sisters. I grew up in a strongly religious family that held up nuns and priests as very special people. When I finished school, I wanted to be around these women. I hoped that maybe a little of their holiness would rub off on me. I've been here for several years and have worked with many sisters. I've learned that they *are* special people. I don't know how much of their holiness has rubbed off on to me! I've also learned that lots of people are special, their dedication and care—not their titles—make them special.
>
> When I first came here, there were lots of sisters everywhere. There's only one here now. For a while I worried about that. But then I realized that the values and the dreams of the sisters were also my values and dreams. A lot of us here feel that way. I guess that if this place is to continue to be a special place, it'll be because of me and others like me. It's up to me to continue the tradition. That's scary. It's also exciting. I think we can do it. I think we *have* to do it. Our people need us.

Conversion is a call to belong, a call to ownership; turning from passive following, turning toward committed leadership. The call to conversion can be a gradual one. It can lead us from viewing healthcare strictly as a career to recognizing its potential holiness.

> I came to work here because the pay was good, the job was challenging, the position would look good on my resume. It was a good career move. I found things here I never expected to see. People really care about each other. They care about the patients and their families. I remember one day being in the emergency room on business when they brought in a young man in cardiac arrest. He died. His mother was with him. The ER was in chaos, all kinds of people were coming in: accidents, gunshot wounds,

broken limbs ... and there was this poor mother all alone. I had the keys to one of the offices down there. I opened it up and took her in there for some peace and quiet. I didn't know what to say to her, or how to help her. I just sat with her for a while and then helped her make some telephone calls. Later, she thanked me and said that I had given her comfort at a terrible moment. I had gone down there to question the ER's accounting procedures!

I've seen miracles happen here. I've also seen death and sorrow. I feel like I'm a part of it all. I've been here 15 years now ... I don't think I could work anywhere else.

COMMUNITY

The call to conversion inevitably leads to a call to care for each other. The gospels rarely show Jesus alone or with one other person. Usually he is surrounded by crowds, and the crowds contain all types of people. Women and men who would not normally be together are brought together by the presence of Emmanuel in their midst. When they see that Jesus helps the suffering ones among them, they are moved to join together to bring the sick and the suffering to him. Many gospel texts tell us about those who brought "all the sick" to Jesus for healing. Luke provides us with a typical scene: "Now when the sun was setting, all those who had any that were sick with various diseases brought them to him; and he laid his hands on every one of them and healed them" (Lk 4:40).

Mark recounts an event that reveals the lengths to which people went to help their friends (Mk 2:1-12; see also Lk 5:17-26). Jesus was "at home," and great crowds had come to hear him teach. The house was filled; even the door was blocked. Four men came to the house carrying a paralyzed person. When they could not get near Jesus, they used great ingenuity. They climbed up onto the roof of the house, removed some of the roof, and lowered the paralytic down into Jesus' presence.

Jesus seemed to appreciate this gesture. He recognized the friends' faith. "And when he saw their faith, he said to the paralytic, 'My son, your sins are forgiven'" (Mk 2:5). A controversy ensued. How could Jesus dare to say that he could forgive sins? Only God can do that! To show that his power was the power of God, Jesus told the paralytic to "rise, take up your pallet, and go home" (Mk 2:11). The former paralytic immediately did so, to the crowd's amazement.

This was indeed a remarkable event. What is more remarkable, however, is that the faith of the man's *friends* prompted his cure. They believed Jesus could cure, and they went to great lengths to see that their friend was helped. They earned Jesus' praise and their friend's healing.

In another case, a mother's care for her daughter prompts her to go to great lengths as well (Mk 7:24-30; Mt 15:21-28). This woman, a Syrophoenician or a Canaanite, enters a home where Jesus is a guest. She goes where she does not belong and speaks to someone she should not address.[5] Her daughter, we are told, "has a demon." She asks Jesus to heal the child. Jesus responds with a rather harsh statement: ". . . it is not right to take the children's bread and throw it to the dogs." Because the child is not a child of Israel, she is to be denied healing. The mother, however, does not take "no" for an answer. She insists, ". . . but even the dogs under the table eat the children's crumbs." Jesus, responding to her faith and her bold courage, tells her that her child is healed.

Once again we see that when divine power is present, when the possibility for healing appears in a people's midst, people are moved to act for the sake of others: for their friends, for their children, for the people of their villages and towns. The same movements are active in our contemporary experience.

The hospital had just been taken over by a different group of sponsors. It was now part of a multi-institutional system. The morale was very low and staff persons were worried. They suspected that the new owners would bring in their own people and that many already there would lose their jobs. Staff didn't trust the new owners and were actively looking for other positions. A new chief operating officer arrived from the system office. For many, he represented the enemy. Two days after he arrived, a hurricane hit the city. The new chief operating officer acted swiftly, intelligently, and with sensitivity. He made room in the hospital for those who needed shelter, especially any employees and their families. He provided assistance to those in emergencies. He was in the midst of the staff, working constantly to keep the hospital open and functioning. A few days after the hurricane, the staff of the hospital took out an ad in the local newspaper. They thanked the new administration and the new sponsors. They said they were proud and grateful to be a part of the new system family.

The sensitivity and tenderness and courage that can appear at the heart of chaos remind us of a caring Savior who hears a cry for help in the midst of the noisy crowd. When someone is moved to care for others, others begin to care in turn. Grace acts when people care; it gives strength and energy where there seemed to have been none. One of the major reasons for such action lies in God's presence engendering hope.

HOPE

Jesus' words and deeds gave rise to great hope among those who longed for God's action in their lives. The gospels are filled with questions, especially questions concerning the identity of Jesus. Perhaps the most telling and most poignant is: "Can this be the one who will save us?" or, as the Samaritan woman says in the gospel of John, "Can this be the Christ?" (Jn 4:28).

The people of Jesus' time knew they had been chosen by God. They were the descendants of Abraham and Sarah and of Moses. They were the inheritors of the covenant and the promised land. Their history told them that God had been faithful to the covenant and true to the promises made to them. Yet all was not well with them. Many were poor, many suffered, their land was occupied by a foreign power, and their leaders were ineffectual and often uncaring. When God's power appeared in their midst to heal and to proclaim good news, they were able to say that God had not forgotten the promise. They hoped; they looked to the future with expectation rather than dread.

The hope that Jesus brought was at once more humble and more magnificent than anyone had dreamed. It was more humble because it did not entail a great, visible political transformation. It was more magnificent because it was one of forgiveness for all, healing for all, eternal life for all.

Hope is a dynamic, brave virtue. Hope relies on the truth of the past and risks the unknown of the future. Without a future, people cannot hope; without a past, people have no basis for hope. The pictures and statues in healthcare facilities' entrances remind us to hope.

Our institution faced a serious crisis. We had to make a decision that would affect our survival. We were not sure we would even *have* a future. Many of us were paralyzed and unable to decide what to do. One day, at one of our meetings, somebody started remembering. She talked about the "old days," and about previous crises—everything from the depression to the fire we'd had to the strike we'd struggled through. Something happened among us. We began to realize that we had survived a lot of hard times, and that we had even become better because of them. We came to see that the institution was bigger than any one person, that the work we did was more important than any single group. We might not survive but the work would. Gradually a new energy entered our discussions, creative ideas seemed to come from nowhere. We made a decision, we took a big risk and it worked. We're still here and the work goes on, and people are being cared for.

God's presence can be felt when people are led to hope. When a people remembers the blessings of its past and the fidelity that those blessings manifest, there is reason to trust in a future. There is not only reason, but also energy and courage to help in the shaping of that future.

THE HOLY GROUND OF HEALTHCARE

All human life is filled with "the grandeur of God." All human experience contains the potential for revelation, for receptivity to grace. The dynamic of giving and receiving care when one is ill, troubled, or suffering is a significant part of human experience. It is, therefore, grace-filled, a holy ground. Healthcare is about people, people who are vulnerable and anxious and people who seek to alleviate suffering, to heal, and to accompany others in their struggles. As one chief executive officer said, "We touch people at the most vulnerable points in their lives—when they're being born, when they're sick, when they're dying." The world of healthcare is unique and intense. Thus, the potential for revelation is also unique and intense. Healthcare is, as we have said, sacred work; it approaches the most basic issues of human experience and seeks to give these meaning and dignity. The ground on which persons devoted to healthcare walk is very holy ground. It is a place to take off our shoes, even as we enter its buildings.

Healthcare is holy ground. It is a place of healing and of suffering, of risk and of care. It is where the divine is revealed in the events of our lives. Moses led an extraordinary life; he saw and spoke with God. Jesus made all life extraordinary; he showed us that God speaks to all of us. Founders and foundresses, pioneers and visionaries—all these remind us of the sacred in our work. Every day we hear a whisper: "Take off your shoes, my friend, this is holy ground."

Notes

1. *The Dynamics of Catholic Identity in Healthcare: A Working Document,* Catholic Health Association, St. Louis, 1987, pp. 40-41.
2. Leonardo Boff, *Liberating Grace,* trans. by John Drury, Orbis Books, Maryknoll, NY, 1979, p. 3.
3. Gerard Manley Hopkins, "God's Grandeur," *Gerard Manley Hopkins: Poems and Prose,* Penguin Books, New York, 1953, p. 27.
4. The young man was tending another man's pigs. Pigs were considered unclean and forbidden by Jewish law. We know, then, that the son was in a totally alien place. See Bernard Brandon Scott, *Hear Then the Parable: A Commentary on the Parables of Jesus,* Augsburg Fortress Press, Minneapolis, 1989, p. 114.
5. In the culture of Jesus' time, women were not expected to participate in gatherings of men and were not allowed to address men directly.

2

"And They All Were Astonished"

THE MISSION AND MINISTRY OF JESUS

Lobbies and waiting rooms tell us much about healthcare institutions and the people they serve. Some are noisy and crowded, filled with people who look worried, tired, or in pain. Others are less crowded, and the people in them appear to be more secure and less frightened. All these places serve as temporary shelters for people who are in need or who keep vigil for their loved ones. The atmosphere in them frequently indicates the urgency of need and the quality of response. People come to healthcare institutions for help. Although they often come in fear and in pain, they also come with hope. They wait in lobbies and other rooms to hear if their hope is justified, if help can be given to them. Sometimes help comes in the form of the curing of an illness; sometimes it appears as sensitivity and caring. Help must be given. That is why people are there, why those lobbies and waiting rooms exist. They are extensions of the mission of healthcare: to give help to those in need.

THE HEALING ACTIVITY OF JESUS

The gospels are filled with types of lobbies and waiting rooms. Sometimes these are open fields or town squares. In other cases, they are crowded houses or small rooms. In all of them, however, people are waiting for help. In all of them, help is given, for these waiting rooms are illuminated by Jesus' presence.

Undoubtedly, people came to Jesus for help and received it. The gospels overflow with healing. All types of people came to Jesus for help: blind beggars, lepers, fathers for their sons, mothers for their daughters, leaders for their servants. They came for all forms of help: freedom from demons, recognition of worth, acceptance, blessing, healing. To all who came, Jesus always gave help. Jesus' healing activity is central in the community's memory of him. Two verses in the gospel of Matthew underscore this. At the beginning of Jesus' public ministry, Matthew writes a brief verse that summarizes Jesus' activity: "And he went about all Galilee, teaching in their synagogues and preaching the gospel of the kingdom *and healing every disease and every infirmity among the people*" (Mt 4:23). Matthew then spends five chapters showing how this verse is true. Chapters 5 to 7, the Sermon on the Mount, contain Jesus' teaching. Chapters 8 to 9 contain a series of healings. At the end of Chapter 9, another brief summary verse appears. In combination with Mt 4:23, it functions as a sort of bracket, a conclusion to a major section of the gospel. The verse is almost identical to 4:23: "And Jesus went about all the cities and villages, teaching in their synagogues and preaching the gospel of the kingdom, *and healing every disease and every infirmity*" (Mt 9:35).

Healing, therefore, is an essential part of Jesus' work. But *why* did Jesus heal so many and so often? We know that he was a very compassionate person and that he took pity on those who suffered. Luke, for example, provides us with a scene that typifies Jesus' compassion (Lk 7:11-17). Jesus entered the city of Nain, and near the gates of the city, he encountered a funeral procession. The dead man was a widow's only son. Jesus saw the widow, had compassion on her, approached her, and told her, "Do not weep." He then went to the bier, touched it, called the young man back to life, and "gave him to his mother." Jesus saw a grieving woman and acted to comfort her. He did not wait to be asked. His compassion was filled with power; it returned a man to life. It is not surprising that those who witnessed this event cried out, "God has visited his people!"

If Jesus healed only because he was a compassionate person, we would look to him as model and example and nothing more. However, there is a deeper, more profound meaning to Jesus' healing activity. The crowd who witnessed the raising of the widow's son recognized this when they cried out that God had visited the people. Jesus' compassion is manifestation of God's activity. If we would touch into the deeper meaning of Jesus' healing, it is necessary to view his actions in relation to his words. Jesus' proclamation and his action form a unified whole.

JESUS AND THE KINGDOM OF GOD

The gospels tell us that Jesus was "sent." Jesus' existence had a purpose. He had a mission in his life, a reason for being and acting as he did. Jesus' purpose, the reason why he was sent by God, was his mission. This mission both governed and colored all that he said and did. Jesus' ministry, his words and his deeds, was the way in which he carried out his mission. If we are to understand the place of healing in Jesus' ministry, we need to understand his mission.

Matthew's summary verses say that Jesus healed every disease and infirmity *and* that he proclaimed the gospel of the kingdom. It is only in terms of this proclamation that we can begin to understand fully the significance of Jesus' healing.

> Jesus appeared as one who proclaimed the Kingdom; all else in his message and ministry serves a function in relation to that proclamation and derives its meaning from it. The challenge to discipleship, the ethical teaching, the disputes about oral tradition or ceremonial law, even the pronouncement of forgiveness of sins and the welcoming of the outcast in the name of God—all these are to be understood in the context of the Kingdom proclamation or they are not to be understood at all.[1]

The "kingdom of God" is a phrase that held great meaning for Jesus' contemporaries. It holds less immediate meaning for us today. For Jesus' contemporaries, the kingdom of God was a symbolic phrase. It summed up both Israel's history and Israel's hope for the future. "Kingdom" points to God's relationship with the people: God reigns over the people as protector and as judge. The kingdom is neither a place nor a description of a societal organization. It is, rather, *activity.* The people of Jesus' time knew themselves as God's people, brought into existence by God's intervention in the Exodus and sustained by God's continuing merciful presence and activity. They awaited God's final intervention that would make the kingdom complete and fully visible.

In the midst of such expectation, Jesus appeared and declared that "the kingdom of God is at hand" (see Mt 4:17; Mk 1:15). It is difficult for us to imagine how dramatic and powerful that statement would have been. The word "gospel" means good news, since the news Jesus proclaimed was what Israel had been anticipating for centuries. Our contemporary culture, with its penchant for instant communication, has diminished somewhat the impact and the power of truly good news. Truly good news frees people and leads them to celebration. People in waiting rooms sometimes have this experience.

M y best friend was diagnosed with uterine cancer a year ago. She had surgery followed by radiation treatment. She was told she needed no more treatment and had begun to feel "normal" again when she discovered a lump in her breast. Her doctor told her they needed to do an immediate biopsy. She was terrified, and so were all her friends and family. After her first experience with cancer, I think we all feared the worst this time. I went to the hospital the morning of the biopsy and waited with her until they took her to surgery. I will never forget the terror in her eyes as they took her away. I waited several hours in the waiting room. During that time, I tried to pray, I tried to think positive thoughts, but mostly I just worried and thought about the long road of suffering ahead for my friend. Finally, the doctor called the waiting room. The lump was benign! My friend would be fine! I was so filled with relief, I didn't know what to do. I was crying and laughing. I knew I should call people, but I was too excited even to speak. I finally called the communications center, and told them the good news. A few more people were laughing and crying. I then decided I would go out and get some flowers for my friend's room (I wanted to buy a whole florist's shop, I was so excited). As I entered the lobby of the hospital, I met another friend who had come there directly from work. I told her the good news, and we embraced and danced together all through the lobby of that hospital. People probably thought we were a little bizarre, but we didn't care. What else could we do with such good news?

Of such wonder is the good news of the proclamation of the kingdom of God. It is not surprising that people followed Jesus, were astonished at what he said, and cried out that God had visited the people. God's reign had finally appeared. However, the story is somewhat more complicated. Many people had definite expectations concerning God's reign. For them, God's intervention would result in the lifting of the oppression under which Israel labored and the restoration of Israel's glory. Even Jesus' disciples expected this, and after the resurrection, when they were reunited with the risen Christ, "they asked him, 'Lord, will you at this time restore the kingdom to Israel?'" (Acts 1:6).

Jesus proclaimed the kingdom, but the kingdom Jesus proclaimed was different than what was expected. One of the best ways to understand this is to listen to Jesus' parables. The parables are stories Jesus told to speak about the kingdom. They are a unique type of story. Although they always deal with very ordinary realities,[2] the parables always contain an element that turns the story and shocks those who listen to it. They tell us that the world (and God's kingdom) is not what we thought it would be. The way parables "work" is the way God's reign works. Let us hear a parable: "He said therefore, 'What is the kingdom of God like? And to what shall I compare it? It is like a grain of mustard seed which a man took and sowed in his garden; and it grew and became a tree, and the birds of the air made nests in its branches'" (Lk 13:18-19).

This parable begins with a very common experience: a man plants his garden. The parable soon becomes complicated, however; mustard seeds were not to be planted in gardens.[3] Mustard grew wild and was very difficult to contain. Why would anyone plant this in a garden? The seed grew and, in the Lukan version, became a tree, but a mature mustard plant was a bush or a shrub. In the parable, the birds make nests in the mustard bush/tree. For Jesus' listeners, the reference to the birds making nests in the tree would have immediately provoked echoes of references to the mighty cedar of Lebanon, an image of the greatness for which Israel believed itself destined. However, now the mighty cedar is transformed into a mustard bush, which is planted in a place it does not belong. Can it be that God's saving intervention happens in unexpected places and with less grandeur than we expected? Is this what it is like when God's reign appears? Does it appear in crowded waiting rooms as well as board rooms or operating rooms?

It is within this larger context, therefore, that Jesus' healing activity begins to take on its full significance. What Jesus said in proclamation and in parable became visible in what he did, especially healing the sick. When paralyzed persons stand and walk, when mourning people are given cause to rejoice, when the leper is cleansed, and when the hemorrhaging woman is healed, we are allowed to see the kingdom of God. God's saving intervention in Jesus Christ means that people are made whole. Jesus healed because he was faithful to his mission. He was unable *not* to heal.[4] To do so would be to hide God's power.

Jesus' disciples knew they were called to share in his mission. Their ministry was the continuation of his: "And preach as you go, saying, 'The kingdom of heaven is at hand.' Heal the sick, raise the dead, cleanse lepers, cast out demons" (Mt 10:7-8). "'Truly, truly, I say to you, the one who believes in me will also do the works that I do; and greater works than these will that one do . . .'" (Jn 14:12). Believers and disciples have continued to know they are called to share in the mission of Jesus Christ. Throughout the history of Christianity, women and men have continued to proclaim the good news of God's reign and have continued to heal the sick, cleanse lepers, and cast out demons. From the first disciples, who healed a paralytic at the Beautiful Gate in Jerusalem (Acts 3:1-10), to the early places of *hospitalitas,* to the leper colonies, to the sisters who nursed the wounded soldiers on battlefields, to today, the power of God's Spirit and the healing mercy of God's kingdom have been revealed.

One woman's courage and ingenuity embodies the revelation of mercy of so many others throughout the centuries. In 1891, Mother Francesca Cabrini was asked to send some of her sisters to serve in a hospital founded by the Scalabrinian Fathers for Italian immigrants in New York City. She agreed, but it was not an easy task.

The Scalabrinian Fathers, though zealous, were grossly inept with the management of the little 109th Street hospital. They provided their occasional eloquent presence and little else, quite expecting the Missionary Sisters of the Sacred Heart, and heaven, to do all the work and pay all the bills. The sisters were under the impossible handicap of having to take unconstructive orders, and besides actually working and running the hospital, were obliged to go out in the streets to beg for the means to live and try to pay the hospital's mounting expenses.

Upon arriving from New Orleans Francesca found the hospital in bankruptcy and about to be discontinued. She would not abandon the merciful project begun by the Scalabrinian Fathers, nor would she submit to their incompetent authority. She sternly refused to assume the debts incurred by them.

She quickly rented two old attached residential buildings on Twelfth Street. After paying the first month's rent she had enough money left to buy ten beds and the materials to make mattresses and sheets.

On October 17, 1892, she moved her ten patients to 12th Street. The patients, some of whom were incurably ill, were jovial and festive in spite of the absolutely strained circumstance of their new hospital. To foil the watching creditors, they crammed all the towels, sheets, and other small articles they could appropriate into their hospital gowns and under the blankets of the stretchers, to take to their new home.[5]

Mother Cabrini found a way to continue her hospital; she *made* ways to continue the ministry of healthcare to those in need.

JESUS AS HEALER

The ministry of healthcare is participation in the mission of Jesus Christ. It is an essential component of the mission common to all believers: proclaiming and making visible God's reign. If we are to continue Jesus' mission, we must reflect on how he carried out that mission. How did he heal? What characterized his healing activity? We could consider many aspects, but three are particularly significant for those who seek to heal in a complex, technological age. Jesus *touched* those he healed; he *listened* to those who called out to him; and he *restored* the suffering to community.

ONE WHO TOUCHES TO HEAL

Jesus lived in a culture that did not value public displays of affection. Strict rules of social interaction prevailed. Men and women did not speak to each other in public, even husband and wife. Children had no voice, and slogans such as "Have you hugged your kid today?" would have been met with horror. In addition, both social and religious rules existed concerning what one could or could not touch. To touch something/someone considered unclean was to become unclean oneself. Lepers were, of course, unclean, as were the dead. A menstruating woman was unclean. In each case, contact with such persons demanded an elaborate ritual of purification.[6] However, Jesus touched lepers, he touched the dead, and he was sensitive to a menstruating woman's touch.

Many scholars have written about the "domestication of the scriptures."[7] We hear the stories again and again, they become very familiar to us, and they no longer surprise or astonish us as they did those who saw and heard Jesus (for example, see Mk 7:37). We accept that Jesus frequently touched the people he healed, but within his cultural milieu, this was truly astonishing.

The gospels further tell us that Jesus' touch was powerful and that people sought to touch and be touched by him because his power healed them. "And all the crowd sought to touch him, for power came forth from him and healed them all" (Lk 6:19). Jesus' touch, filled with healing power, was manifestation of God's power. It was also manifestation of God's involvement in the suffering of human beings. Jesus the healer did not stand at a distance from those who needed him; he did not merely "lift a finger" and cure the lame, the leper, and the bent woman. He waded into crowds, went to people's homes, drew near, touched others, and allowed himself to be touched. He was irresistibly drawn to those in need.

Healthcare today is an amazing complex of scientific and technological brilliance. Our capacities for diagnosis and treatment have been enhanced a hundredfold, but it is still about people and touching people to heal them. Unfortunately, this fact is sometimes lost. The complexities of treatment, the stress of overwork, and sheer numbers of patients on any given day can often lead healthcare givers to lose sight of the importance of a caring, reverential touch. One author describes in a work of fiction what is often the case in reality.

> Lila feels as though she has been left out in a field for the buzzards. The nurses are in at all hours, making no special effort to be quiet—a nurse who checks dressings, another one who changes dressings, a nurse with blood-thinner shots three times a day, a nurse with breathing-machine treatments, various nurses' aides who check temperature and blood pressure, the cleaning woman, the mail lady, the priest and nuns from the

hospital, the girls who fill the water jugs, the woman who brings the meal trays, the candy stripers selling toiletries and candy and magazines from a cart. Lila can't keep track of all the nurses who come to check her drainage tube—squirting the murky fluid out of the plastic collection bottle, measuring the fluid intake and output, writing on charts. The nurses walk her around the entire third floor, twice a day, accompanied by her I.V. bag, wheeling on a stand.[8]

Lila, although surrounded by people who are caring for her, "feels as though she has been left out in a field for the buzzards." A consciousness of the importance of the way one checks dressings, changes them, checks drainage tubes, and walks with a patient can help to remind us of the gospel, which grounds all that we do. This was the case for another woman who accompanied her mother as she was undergoing a series of tests.

M y mother was in the hospital with a broken hip. She was in a lot of pain and was quite disoriented. The doctor ordered some x-rays. When they came to get her, the attendants treated her like she was a sack of potatoes. Then, when we got down to the x-ray department, she had to wait a long time. She was still in pain, and she kept saying she was cold. Finally, someone came out from the lab with a blanket. He covered my mother with great gentleness and care. It was a simple act, but one done with such reverence that my mother was not only warmed but also comforted. She relaxed, smiled, and even began to doze off.

A gentle touch is a powerful touch. It carries within itself the possibility for healing and for revelation.

ONE WHO LISTENS TO THE VOICE OF SUFFERING

Another striking aspect of Jesus' healing activity is his insistence on listening to those who were suffering. We are often told in the gospels that the disciples did not fully understand Jesus. They often seem much more concerned for order than he is. Several times in the gospels, situations get a little "messy," and the disciples try to avoid scenes. At one point, mothers bring their children to Jesus, and the disciples try to stop them. Jesus rebukes the disciples and takes the children into his arms and blesses them (Mk 10:13-16). Another time, a foreign woman enters a dinner uninvited. She argues with Jesus concerning her daughter's healing. The disciples tell Jesus to get rid of her because she is causing a scene. Jesus does the opposite, and the daughter is healed of her demon (Mt 15:22-28).

In another case, the crowds themselves rebuke those who cry out. Matthew tells us that Jesus had left the town of Jericho and was walking along the road surrounded by a great crowd. Two blind men were sitting by the side of the road. When they heard that it was Jesus who was passing by, they cried out, "Have mercy on us, Son of David." The crowds rebuked the blind men, but these persistent needy ones only cried out louder. Jesus stopped and engaged the men in conversation. He asked them what they needed, what was wrong with them. He listened to their request that their eyes be opened; he touched their eyes, and they saw (Mt 20:29-34).

Jesus was able to hear the cries of people even when others tried to silence them. He was free to listen to them, stop what he was doing, and take a detour on his road because he was needed. God's power in Jesus pays attention to the suffering and listens for its voice.

Today's healthcare world is marked by a highly technical language. Often the patient cannot understand what is said. Often, too, what the patient says is not heard. Lila, recovering from a mastectomy, experiences this. When her physician enters her room after her surgery, he tells her that they discovered cancer in two of the lymph nodes they had removed.

. . . L ila's head spins as the doctor explains that once the cancer has reached the lymph nodes, it has gone into the bloodstream, and then it can end up anywhere. The news doesn't quite register.

"I'm recommending chemotherapy," the doctor says.

"Is that cobalt?" Lila asks weakly . . .

The doctor says, "No. This will be a combination of three drugs— Cytoxan, methotrexate and 5FU." He explains that she will have a chart showing two weeks of treatments, then a three-week rest period, then two weeks of treatments, and so on. She will get both pills and shots. Like dogs teaming up on a rabbit, Cat and Nancy (Lila's daughters) jump on him about side effects.

"This particular treatment is tolerated very well," he says. "That's not to say there won't be side effects. A little hair loss, a little nausea. Some people react more adversely than others."

Lila can't keep her mind on what he's saying. "I've got plenty of hair," she says, tugging at her curls.[9]

Lila is not able to hear the physician, and he does not make it easy for her to do so. He explains her treatment to her in technical language and does not check to see if the news has "registered." We are a long way from the sensitive listening and speaking of Jesus. Lila's experience was not that of the kingdom of God. The story of Lila is not the only way one experiences healthcare, however; the fictitious physician in her story does not represent all physicians.

Another physician explains how he learned the importance of listening very early in his career and how he learned this from his patients.

T he first patient was a pathetic seven-year-old girl who had been badly burned over most of her body. She had to undergo a daily ordeal of a whirlpool bath during which the burnt flesh was tweezered away from her raw, open wounds. This experience was horribly painful to her. She screamed and moaned and begged the medical team, whose efforts she stubbornly fought off, not to hurt her any more. My job as a neophyte clinical student was to hold her uninjured hand, as much to reassure and calm her as to enable the surgical resident to quickly pull away the dead, infected tissue in the pool of swirling water, which rapidly turned pinkish, then bloody red. Clumsily, with a beginner's uncertainty of how to proceed, I tried to distract this little patient from her traumatic daily confrontation with terrible pain. I tried talking to her about her home, her family, her school—almost anything that might draw her attention away from her suffering .... Then one day, I made contact. At wit's end, angered at my own ignorance and impotence, uncertain what to do besides clutching the small hand, and in despair over her unrelenting anguish, I found myself asking her to tell me how she tolerated it, what the feeling was like of being so badly burned and having to experience the awful surgical ritual, day after day after day. She stopped, quite surprised, and looked at me from a face so disfigured it was difficult to read the expression; then, in terms direct and simple, she told me. While she spoke, she grasped my hand harder and neither screamed nor fought off the surgeon or the nurse.... She taught me a grand lesson in patient care: that it is possible to talk with patients, even those who are most distressed, about the actual experience of illness, and that witnessing and helping to order that experience can be of therapeutic value.[10]

Listening, and listening carefully, is an integral part of healing. When we listen to another's pain or fear, we participate in Jesus' healing activity, we set free God's loving mercy.

ONE WHO RESTORES RELATIONSHIPS

Jesus touched those he healed; he listened to their pain. His healing power healed hearts as well as bodies. It also restored relationships. Illness and pain isolate people. They often imprison a person in her or his own suffering. This was especially true of many persons in Jesus' culture. Lepers were isolated, as were those suffering from other diseases. Jesus' healing eased the isolation; it effected healing for families and friends as well.

There are several stories in the gospels when parents go to Jesus seeking help for their children. In all these cases, Jesus heals the child. Mark offers a particularly poignant account (Mk 9:14-29; see also Lk 9:37-42). A young boy is possessed by a demon that throws him "into the fire and into the water to destroy him." The father has taken his child to the disciples, but they are unable to cure him. He then goes to Jesus and says, "If you can do anything, have pity on us and help us." Jesus reminds the father that all things are possible for the one who believes. The father cries, "I believe; help my unbelief!" Jesus then commands the demon to leave the boy. As it does so, it renders the child unconscious. The people think he is dead, but Jesus takes him by the hand and raises him up. The child is freed, and so is the father. Jesus' compassionate healing extends to those who suffer with others as well as to those in their own agony. Father and son are able to relate to each other now; they can function in their roles within the community. When God's saving power touches a child, it also touches those who care for the child.

The scriptures also talk much about lepers. They, the unclean, approach Jesus quite frequently and ask him to make them whole. Jesus does. He sometimes tells them that they should go to the priest and make an offering (Mt 8:5). The leper had to do this, not because one "paid a fee" for a cure, but because it was through the certification by a priest that one was declared clean and thus able to rejoin the community. Jesus made the lepers' bodies whole, and he restored them to full belonging among their people.

Jesus' compassion, manifestation of God's own healing power, shows itself in a touch that heals, a heart that listens, and a healing that restores relationships. When people involved in healthcare are attentive to relationships they also manifest God's power. Perhaps the "place" where this is most significant today is in our treatment of persons with AIDS (acquired immunodeficiency syndrome). Relationships are absolutely vital for those who face a painful death, but sometimes medical care only intensifies the isolation. At other times, it blessedly relieves it. Two accounts permit us to see both aspects of this.

A physician recounts the experience of "Horacio Grippa," a homosexual teacher with AIDS. He has lost his job, been evicted from his apartment, and been rejected by his parents. He describes his experience in a hospital.

> The nurses are scared of me; the doctors wear masks and sometimes gloves. Even the priest doesn't seem too anxious to shake my hand. What the hell is this? I'm not a leper. Do they want to lock me up and shoot me? I've got no family, no friends. Where do I go? What do I do? God, this is horrible!

Is He punishing me? The only thing I got going for me is that I'm not dying—at least, not yet.[11]

Horacio is clearly an angry, suffering person. His isolation is almost total. Unfortunately, he has not been able to meet and be touched by the one who says, "Of course I want to heal you." Another person did meet such an individual, a member of a pastoral care team. He was able to move from isolation to restoration.

"Michael Jones" was a 34-year-old museum curator on the West Coast. When Michael's physician diagnosed Michael's symptoms as ARC (AIDS related complex), Michael "responded with self-isolation. He sometimes missed work for days at a time because of physical symptoms or depression. Michael felt a loss of contact with others from then on, making few attempts to keep in touch with friends and feeling that they made few attempts to keep in touch with him."[12]

When Michael's symptoms intensified, he flew to a hospital in the Midwest, where he demanded anonymity. No one in the waiting room waited for Michael. A member of the pastoral care team gradually came to know Michael and established a relationship. Michael gradually moved out of his isolation into trust and reconciliation. When he was discharged from the hospital, he decided to return home. The hospital chaplain found a support group for Michael in his hometown. Michael was no longer alone. The support persons in Michael's town helped him to reestablish contact with the most significant person in Michael's life. This person travelled several thousand miles to be with him and cared for him until he died.

The care Michael received is the care of the gospel. It is a care filled with compassion, one that reaches out to restore belonging. This type of care shows us what happens when God reigns.

People in lobbies and waiting rooms tend to remember. As they await the news, they look back to the events and times that brought them to this moment. The Catholic healthcare ministry of the twentieth and twenty-first centuries must also remember. We are all called to remember the events and the times that have brought us to the present. At the heart of these events is one filled with the power of God, who proclaimed good news and showed us what happened when good news came true. All who share in the healthcare ministry share in that proclamation, that revelation, that power. How can we not be astonished?

Notes

1. Norman Perrin, *Rediscovering the Teaching of Jesus,* Harper & Row Publishers, Inc., New York, 1976, p. 54.
2. See Chapter 1, pp. 7-9 for a discussion on the importance of the ordinary in Jesus' words and actions.
3. Bernard Brandon Scott, *Hear Then the Parable: A Commentary on the Parables of Jesus,* Augsburg Fortress Press, Minneapolis, 1989, pp. 373-387.
4. It must be noted that moments occur in the gospel when Jesus could not heal (see Mt 13:53-58; Mk 6:4-6). Jesus could not heal in these cases because the people rejected him and thus rejected the saving power of God's kingdom.
5. Pietro Di Donato, *The Immigrant Saint: The Life of Mother Cabrini,* McGraw-Hill Book Co., New York, 1960, pp. 102-103.
6. See Leviticus, Chapters 11 to 15, for descriptions of what is unclean and what is clean. These chapters also describe some of the purification rituals.
7. Robin Scroggs, for example, says that modern Christianity has lost much of the power of Pauline writings because they are so familiar. They no longer shock us as they should. Robin Scorggs, *Paul for a New Day,* Fortress Press, Philadelphia, 1977, p. 3.
8. Bobbie Ann Mason, *Spence + Lila,* Harper & Row Publishers, Inc., New York, 1977, p. 61.
9. Mason, pp. 62-63.
10. Arthur Kleinman, *The Illness Narratives: Suffering, Healing and the Human Condition,* Basic Books, Inc., New York, 1988, pp. xii-xiii.
11. Kleinman, pp. 162-163.
12. Mary E. Johnson, "A Case Study in Pastoral Counseling," *Health Progress* May 1986, p. 38.

3

"Everybody Needs a Home"

THE HEALTHCARE MINISTRY AND THE CATHOLIC CHURCH

Anyone who walks through Chicago's O'Hare airport these days encounters a new and disturbing phenomenon. The homeless have come to O'Hare. An extension of the Chicago rapid transit system has made it possible for many who previously were confined in the core city to travel to the airport. They come there for many reasons: it is warm, open 24 hours, and safe. The new faces at the busy airport are disturbing to many. Some complain that the presence of the homeless is frightening for people and that newcomers to the city should not be greeted with such sights. Others say that the homeless disrupt the airport and tax already overburdened services. Still others point out that the *real* disturbance is that there are so many homeless, that so many men, women, and children need to use an airport as their only shelter.

The increase in homeless persons in the United States is one of our most worrisome problems. The increase in homeless families with children is one of our most distressing troubles. To have no home is a terrible thing.

TO HAVE A HOME

Homes represent many things. For most of us, the home is where life takes place, where activities begin and end. It is the place where we are safe, secure in the conviction that the people there will care for us. It is the starting point, the place from which we gradually venture forth into the larger world.

For many, home is often a memory. It is the place where things happened, where we learned, where we laughed and wept. Our childhood homes were the entrance to the world as home. If the family home was warm and safe, we assumed the world as home would also be that way. If the family home was filled with fear and sorrow, we learned to fear a world full of threats.

The homes we have now are expressions of ourselves. They show what is important to us, what we value and cherish. They say to those for whom we care that we promise them shelter and refuge and comfort. They say to the larger world that we are people who are *able* to care for others. Homes are really sacred places where we enact the rituals and the stories of our lives. They are the holy ground where we first and continuously meet God's presence in our lives. Everyone needs a home.

EARLY CHRISTIAN HOUSE CHURCHES

Homes have always been essential. From prehistoric caves with painted walls, to sod houses on the Western plains, to the "starter house," to the palatial mansion, people have always instinctively built homes for themselves and their loved ones. Homes played a very important part in the beginnings of Christianity, since people's homes became the first meeting places for the communities.

The epistles of Paul and the Acts of the Apostles provide us with some glimpses of life among the first Christians. Several passages refer to "the community *(ekklesia)* which meets in the house" of some person (1 Cor 16:19; Rom 16:5; Philemon 2; Col 4:15; Acts 12:12-17).[1] Believers came together in the homes of people such as Prisca and Aquilla, Stephanus, Apphia and Archippus to share in the Lord's Supper, to enjoy fellowship, and to see that the needs of all were addressed. These homes became the first centers of worship, the first places of welcoming for the Christian community. They were also the places from which members were sent forth to proclaim the good news, to care for the poor, and to heal the sick. From these homes, therefore, Christian ministry sprang forth. New Testament texts that describe these house churches tell us that the Christian community remembered them and recognized their value and their importance, even as we remember our first and early homes.

IMAGES OF THE CHURCH

Our culture has many terms and images for houses. The Sunday *New York Times'* real estate section uses such words as "Secluded Hideaway," "Elegant Estate," "Magnificent Apartment," and "Central Park West." More modest advertisements refer to "Starter Home," "Pleasant Surroundings," and "Cozy Studio" or say that a certain place "needs work." Each of these phrases conjures up a myriad of images. Images are basic to our thoughts and aspirations for houses. The same has been and is true of the Church. We use many images. When we talk about Church, we talk first and foremost about a mystery. The Church is a vehicle for the relationship between God and humankind which can never be fully expressed in logical, declarative sentences. Throughout history, people have sought to express that mystery in terms of images that speak to the heart as well as to the mind of the believer.

There are many significant images for the Church. The New Testament contains several, such as the Body of Christ, the new Israel, and the new People of God.[2] The use of images has much to do with people's understanding of themselves, and the importance of various images for Church have always been in relation to the Church's self-understanding at different points in history.[3] Vatican II, for example, stressed the image of Church as the "People of God," whereas earlier writings, especially the papal writings, had spoken of the Church as a "Perfect Society" or as the "Mystical Body of Christ." In their report of the Special Synod of 1985, convoked by Pope John Paul II to reflect on the significance of Vatican II, the bishops speak of the Church as "mystery" and as "communion."

Perhaps another image, that of the early house churches, can provide an important vehicle for the self-understanding of those who seek to serve in the Catholic healthcare ministry and can enable us to express better our relationship to the Church. We might say that the Catholic Church is the "home" of the Catholic healthcare ministry, and everybody needs a home.

As we have seen, the homes of people became the centers for worship, for proclamation, for mutual concern, and for the sending forth of members to serve in the world. In these homes, people struggled to understand who they were and what God asked of them. They were nourished by the Word of God and by the Lord's Supper. They came to know each other and found community and encouragement from each other. They spoke of the community's needs and sent members forth to proclaim and witness to God's power at work in Jesus Christ. The house churches were home for the people: from them they ventured forth in service; to them they went for sustenance, encouragement, community, and wisdom.

The early Christian communities grew quickly and outgrew the houses in which they met. The Church remained home, however, the place where believers belonged, the place from which they were sent forth. Throughout the Church's history, persons have always been sent forth to exercise the ministry of healthcare. Today, although the Catholic Church is a worldwide institution with many buildings, complex structures, and millions of members, the dynamic of the house churches remains. People gather within the Church and come to know who they are; they are sent forth from/by the Church to proclaim the good news, to assist in the mission that gives the Church its identity.

SENT FORTH TO SERVE

Throughout the Church's history, persons have always been sent forth to assist in its mission through the ministry of caring for the needs of others. The Acts of the Apostles (6:1-6) provides us with a glimpse of how this first happened. As the communities grew in numbers, difficulties arose. When the communities would gather to share and to distribute food, some (the "widows of the Hellenists" [Acts 6:1-2]) were being neglected. To address this problem, the community appointed seven members to take care of these others' needs. The community leaders approved the choice and commissioned the seven. As Christianity expanded, persons known as deacons and deaconesses were called forth to care for others. Padberg points out that deacons were to provide "hospitalitas." "Hospitalitas" means much more than "hospitality" does today. "For the always minority and often persecuted Christians of the first centuries it meant help of every kind for their needy sisters and brothers in the faith."[4] Padberg explains that this activity took place in four ways: the establishment of inns for travellers, infirmaries, foundling homes, and homes for the aged. Each of these involved a concern for health, but the inns for travellers and the infirmaries were the forerunners of systematic healthcare. The most important function of the inns was to shelter the sick. Christians continued to provide this shelter for centuries and responded to the needs of pilgrims, soldiers in the Crusades, and all who came to them.

Eventually, religious congregations of men and women assumed responsibility for healthcare institutions. (Women's religious congregations did not become actively involved until after the Reformation, however, because most women's congregations were separated from the world [cloistered] until that time.) Today, most Catholic healthcare facilities in the United States continue to be sponsored by religious congregations, but new, alternative models of sponsorship are being explored. Whether we speak of inns for sick travellers, infirmaries, nursing on the battlefields, acute care hospitals, hospices, or long-term care facilities, we speak of the same reality: care for the needs of our people.

CHURCH AS HOME

The impetus to serve that originated with the early house churches is the same Spirit-filled impetus that we know today. The Church as home continues to inspire us to serve, continues to send us forth in service. But how, we might ask, does the Church continue to be home for us and for the ministry? There are many ways in which this happens, since God's Spirit can never be contained. There are, however, three aspects of special significance: inspiration, recognition, and reminder of the tradition.

INSPIRATION

I'm here because I remember the stories from my childhood. When I was a little girl, the sisters used to tell us about the saints and how they would sacrifice and do brave things. They always stressed how the saints helped other people, how they suffered for the sake of others. Those stories inspired me, they made me want to do great things like the saints had done. I wondered how I could do that, and eventually I became involved in healthcare. I know I'm not a saint, but still I try to be one. I try to be like those great people whose stories I learned as a child. When I get down, when things get to be too much, I talk to the saints, ask them to help me. And they do. The inspiration is still there.

The Catholic Church has an incredibly rich history. This history is peopled with individuals whose lives and works are inspiration and model for all of us. When the Church tells their stories, we are reminded of the people to whom we belong. We are given models to emulate. The Church is more than its history, however, and its capacity to inspire exceeds the lives of the saints. The Catholic Church shares in the great treasure of the scriptures, which have formed it and continue to give it life. When the scriptures are proclaimed, when we are led to explore the mystery of God's word, the richness and the mystery of this word can only give us life and courage. The scriptures are about life and the fundamental human experiences that comprise a life. When proclaimed by the Church, they show us that life involves a relationship to a loving God and membership in a blessed people. Scripture gives us hope, calls us to conversion, and encourages us in sorrow.

> F or in the sacred books, the Father who is in heaven meets His children with great love and speaks with them; and the force and power in the word of God is so great that it remains the support and energy of the Church, the strength of faith for her children, the food of the soul, the pure and perennial source of spiritual life.[5]

All engaged in the ministry of healthcare deal daily with pain, suffering and sorrow. The Church, when it reminds us of our history and when it opens the treasure of God's word, is an inexhaustible source of inspiration.

RECOGNITION

Everybody needs recognition. When we do not receive it, something in us shrivels. When people gather around a table and do not notice the person next to them, the meal is spoiled. When patients feel they are only an interesting case, the suffering intensifies.

Recognition that we are, that we are human, and that we are significant persons is vital to our own self-understanding. Recognition by those closest to us is most vital. It is one thing to be disregarded by strangers, but another to be ignored in one's own home. Further, recognition and appreciation of the work we do, and the contributions we make encourage us and enhance our ability to be creative and effective. The event in the Acts of the Apostles wherein "the Seven" were called forth to serve tells us that these seven were recognized and affirmed by the community and its leaders. The Church continues such recognition today. At times, this recognition is formal. The bishops, responsible for the ministries in their respective dioceses, officially recognize those works that are truly expressive of the church's mission. The U.S. bishops offered such recognition in their 1981 statement, *Health and Health Care*. They declared that one purpose for the statement was their desire "to express our full commitment to the Catholic health care apostolate and our encouragement and support of professionals in the health field."[6]

A more informal, more pervasive recognition also takes place. This is the acknowledgment by the whole people of God that the ministry of healthcare is indeed a vital part of the Church's activity and that all are called on to support this work. The recent national Commission on Catholic Health Care Ministry made this point very strongly in its report on the future of the ministry. When it describes a vision for the future, a renewed commitment to the ministry by the entire Church is the first element.

> Renewed commitment to the health care ministry by the whole community of believers will be the key to achieving the new vision. In light of the Christian obligation to care for one's neighbor, individual members of the community will be zealous in ministering to the sufferings, disabilities, and frailties of others...
>
> The ecclesial community will play an important role in initiating, evaluating, and coordinating health services. The bishop, who has the oversight of all ministry within a local church, will call others to their responsibility to promote and support the healing ministry...
>
> Catholics will look to their health care institutions and services as public expressions of the Church's commitment to the healing ministry. The religious motives which inspired the founding of health care ministries will continue to animate their stance against the dehumanizing character of much contemporary health care. The Catholic identity of the institutions will not be a weak vestige of an earlier day, but an active force shaping the decisions and actions of trustees, managers, physicians, and employees...
> This renewed commitment to the health care ministry on the part of the whole Church will have broadened and deepened participation in it from all sides, among church leaders and members in general as well as health care professionals.[7]

TRADITION

Inspiration to join in a ministry and recognition and ownership of the ministry belong in the home that is Church. There is yet another aspect to the Church's relation to healthcare. The Church reminds us of its tradition. Tradition is the transmission of what is cherished and believed. All people have traditions, ways to act, values and taboos, and treasured stories, which are handed down from generation to generation. New experiences may shape the expressions of these traditions, but the core remains the same. The Catholic Church also has a tradition, one that comes to us from the Word of God and the understanding of that Word by the Apostles first, then by others through the centuries. "Now what was handed on by the apostles includes everything which contributes to the holiness of life, and the increase in faith of the People of God; and so the Church, in her teaching, life, and worship, perpetuates and hands on to all generations all that she herself is, all that she believes."[8] All who serve in the Catholic healthcare ministry are inheritors of the Church's tradition; all are enriched by it and find their identity in it.

A particularly significant and highly treasured aspect of the Church's tradition is its sacramental nature.

> Sacrament refers to the revelation or mediation of God's presence in the human community through symbolic activity. In fact, Catholics understand Christ, the Church, and themselves as radically sacramental. As sacrament, Christ, the Church, and the lives of Christians are revelatory symbols in that they mediate the reality of God's saving presence among us and invite us to be moved, healed, challenged, and transformed by that presence.[9]

Although we usually associate the Catholic tradition with the seven sacraments, it is important to realize that the Church understands its very being as sacrament. That is, the Church, when true to who she is, reveals and enables encounter with the living God. The celebration of the Church's seven sacraments originates from the nature of Church as sacrament. "The Church crystallizes and celebrates its general sacramental identity in the celebration of seven distinctive events, namely, the seven sacraments. These seven ritual celebrations are intense moments of encounter wherein we respond to the inviting presence of the Lord among us and rejoice in this saving presence as it actually touches us here and now."[10]

The Church's tradition, therefore, helps us to understand who we are and what we are called to be: revealers and mediators of God's saving presence. Healthcare is a uniquely privileged ministry; the compassion of God reaches people through our compassion. The welcoming God welcomes the homeless when we exercise true *hospitalitas*.

> I walked into our hospital lobby one morning. Usually the hospital lobby, having been cleaned during the night, is all bright and sparkling. But this morning it looked like the worst version of a bus station—backpacks everywhere, soda bottles, paper cups. When I went upstairs, I noticed a wing which had been closed for some renovation was opened. I asked around and found out that last night we had admitted a gypsy. His whole clan had come with him, and they wouldn't go home. They wanted to stay. Well, some nurses and workers took some initiative and got the fellow in charge of the facilities to open the temporarily closed wing. They made up the beds and put the gypsies up for the night. Of course, in the morning they were back in the lobby messing it up. It caused a lot of buzzing. But it had its humorous side. It had its compassionate and human side also.

"We are a people of hospitality.... Hospitality is always a sharp ear and fast feet. It entails being attentive and being inventive. Welcoming is important to us. The graciousness of God encourages the graciousness of people."[11] The Catholic Church's understanding of itself as sacrament is the home of the healthcare ministry's identity. Witness to God's unlimited mercy and the presence of God's saving compassion, the ministry of healthcare is sacred, a sacrament of encounter with the divine.

WHAT IS ASKED OF US

Others' expectations and hopes for us first become evident in our homes. We learn appropriate behavior, we absorb attitudes, and we respond (more or less well) to others' demands. We also learn to place expectations on others. The same is true of the Church. It asks things from us; we expect things from it. The Church calls us to fidelity to the tradition. Such fidelity implies a knowledge of that tradition, reflection on its meaning, and attention to how that tradition expresses itself in our times. The tradition is a living reality always moving toward greater fullness. "For, as the centuries succeed one another, the Church constantly moves toward the fullness of divine truth until the words of God reach their complete fulfillment in her."[12] Fidelity to the tradition implies an active participation in the Church's movement toward fulfillment. It implies committed participation in the ongoing search to understand what has been so graciously revealed to God's people.

Further, the Church asks of us a zealous discipleship. The first Christians were sent forth with great enthusiasm. They were to continue the Savior's work; theirs was a blessed activity. The same is true today. Healthcare is an astonishing work; its potential for healing is amazing. When healthcare is also holy work, its potential for healing is beyond imagining. Such holy work will not thrive in lackluster surroundings. It needs courage, commitment, and inventiveness. "Truly, truly, I say to you, the one who believes in me will also do the works that I do; and greater than these will that one do ..." (Jn 14:12).

Finally, those who serve in the ministry of Catholic healthcare are called to continue to reveal God's merciful presence in our world. For how will people know that God is near? How will the suffering know that God goes with them into suffering and even into death unless God's people show them? How will the broken learn that God heals unless others strive to heal?

WHAT WE ASK

What do we ask of the Church? We ask continued inspiration, and greater, more active recognition. We ask that the richness of the Church's tradition be ever more faithfully shared. We ask, finally, for what is fundamental to a home, for what was at the heart of the early Christians' meetings: we ask for nourishment. The Church, as home, must provide food for our journey through its teaching authority, through its transmission of the tradition, and through meaningful celebration of its sacramental life. It must sustain those who dwell in it, it must give sustenance that will strengthen, food that we enjoy even as it appeases our hunger. Everybody needs food; everybody needs a home.

The homeless have come to O'Hare. They remind all who travel through that airport of one of the most shameful aspects of our contemporary society. They remind us that everybody needs a home. They call us to care for and cherish the home we have, even as we struggle to provide homes for those who have none.

Notes

1. For a study of the social world of early Christianity, consult Wayne A. Meeks, *The First Urban Christians: The Social World of the Apostle Paul,* Yale University Press, New Haven, CT, 1983. See also Vincent Branick, *The House Church in the Writings of Paul,* Michael Glazier, Inc., Wilmington, DE, 1989, and Michael H. Crosby, *House of Disciples: Church, Economics, and Justice in Matthew,* Orbis Books, Maryknoll, NY, 1988. Crosby maintains that the image of house is basic to the Matthean gospel.
2. Avery Dulles, in his classic work, *Models of the Church,* Yale University Press, New Haven, CT, 1974, p. 17, cites Paul Minear's listing of 96 images in *Images of the Church in the New Testament,* Westminister Press, Philadelphia, 1960.
3. Dulles provides a summary of the historical uses of images for the Church; see especially Chapter One. See also his later work, *Models of Revelation,* Doubleday Publishing Co., New York, 1985. See also Walter Burghardt, "Models of Church, Models of Health Apostolate," *Hospital Progress,* May, 1981, 35-42.
4. John W. Padberg, "Catholic Health Care—The Mission and the Ministry," *Parameters in Health Care,* Spring 1983, p. 2.
5. "The Dogmatic Constitution on Divine Revelation," no. 21, ed., Walter M. Abbott, *The Documents of Vatican II,* New Century Publishers, Inc., Piscataway, NY, 1966.
6. *Health and Health Care,* National Conference of Catholic Bishops, Washington, DC, 1981, no. 3.

7. *Catholic Health Ministry: A New Vision for a New Century,* The Commission on Catholic Health Care Ministry, Farmington Hills, MI, 1988, pp. 12-13.

8. "The Dogmatic Constitution on Divine Revelation," no. 8.

9. *The Dynamics of Catholic Identity in Healthcare: A Working Document,* Catholic Health Association, St. Louis, 1987, p. 22.

10. *Catholic Identity,* p. 23.

11. Both the account of welcoming the gypsies and the quote are from *Catholic Identity,* pp. 39-40.

12. "The Dogmatic Constitution on Divine Revelation," no. 8.

4

"What Do I Do with All of This Suffering?"

SUFFERING IN THE JUDAIC-CHRISTIAN TRADITION

Anyone who walks through a modern healthcare facility encounters many sights: laboratories, intensive care units, trauma centers, birthing centers, physical therapy equipment, hospice units, pediatric wards, occupational therapy.

Much of what we see in any healthcare facility is amazing, some is perplexing, some is cause for rejoicing, and some is cause for worry. No matter where one goes, one always finds people and always finds suffering. Some suffering is life giving, as that of a woman giving birth (see Jn 16:21). Much suffering can be alleviated, its causes eliminated. Other suffering just seems senseless and cruel. Healthcare is about suffering. It is about tending to persons who are vulnerable, fragile, and in pain. This can be an affirming and even exhilirating experience. It can also be a devastating one.

Modern medicine's ability to alleviate suffering is remarkable. Pain that once was overwhelming can now be eliminated or controlled. Diseases that formerly destroyed a body have been eradicated; methods of dealing with chronic illness have been enhanced. All these advances, and our ability to use them to help others who are suffering, can exhilarate us, and make us justly proud of our skills. At the same time, suffering continues, appearing in new forms and guises that baffle and overwhelm us in their persistence. Sometimes, the world, the people we care for, and ourselves, seem lost in suffering. We are helpless before it, devastated by it.

The woman found herself crying as she walked to her car. She worked in a clinic, serving mothers and young children in an inner-city area. It had been a long day, a typical day. She had seen undernourished children, had tried to explain the principles of nutrition to mothers who had no money, often spoke no English, and mostly were alone in the world. Today had also brought a particularly brutal case of abuse, the culmination of a series of suspected abuses, the culmination of months of fear to speak out, to leave home. Today had also brought more budget cuts. Some staff would have to leave; the rubber band of services would be stretched even farther. At one point during the wearying day, the woman looked at all those waiting for help, all those in pain, and asked herself: "What do I do with all of this suffering? How can I even make a dent? How can I even begin to understand it?" She continued to ask these questions as she walked to her car.

THE RANGE OF SUFFERING

This woman's questions echo in the hearts of everyone who works in healthcare. They are painfully urgent and, for many, ultimately unanswerable. The way we view suffering determines the way we respond to such questions. The meaning we give to it influences what we "do" with it. In the medical world, there is sometimes a tendency to equate suffering with physical pain and to treat suffering by treating pain. Suffering involves much more than physical pain, however, and its power extends beyond the human body to all that is the human person. Suffering attacks the integrity of persons, both those who suffer *and* those who accompany the suffering. Cassel defines suffering as "the state of severe distress associated with events that threaten the intactness of the person."[1]

Cassel enumerates the many aspects that make up the intactness of a person: "the lived past, the family's lived past, culture and society, roles, the instrumental dimension, associations and relationships, the body, the unconcious mind, the political being, the secret life, the perceived future, and the transcendent dimension."[2] Such a listing reminds us of the complexity of suffering and the havoc it wreaks on human lives. It also reminds us that the alleviation of suffering is no easy task.

Simone Weil, philosopher and mystic, knew great suffering in her own life and wrote eloquently of its power. She distinguishes between what she calls "suffering," a purely physical phenomenon that passes, and "affliction," which involves the soul as well as the body. "It takes possession of the soul and marks it through and through with its own particular mark, the mark of slavery."[3] Weil takes us to the heart of the question when she points out that affliction invades and wounds the soul. The person who suffers often experiences a sense of abandonment. People frequently turn from those who suffer, leaving them isolated and alone in their anguish. Suffering involves all human life; it speaks in physical pain, wreaks havoc in the soul, and impairs human relationships. "What do I do with all of this suffering?"

RESPONSES TO SUFFERING

There are as many responses to human suffering as there are human beings. Suffering is a uniquely personal experience that involves the whole person, and only the individual can know his or her own suffering. This is part of the anguish of suffering—it can never be fully shared. Each person responds according to his or her capabilities and resources. Suffering is not, however, a purely individual phenomenon. It affects those whose lives are connected to the suffering one, and it often affects a whole society. The terrible suffering of oppression and poverty, for example, belong to all peoples and must be addressed by all. A particular form of suffering can test the very fabric of a culture; AIDS is but one example of this. The response of the culture shows its compassion, its ability to tolerate diversity, its ingenuity in combatting a terrible disease. Although people must offer their own response to suffering as it touches their lives, our contemporary culture offers some common responses: denial, resistance, and acceptance.[4]

DENIAL

To enter into suffering is a frightening and sobering experience. To see the sufferings of others robs us of our innocence, says Soelle, and forces us to choose. We must either act to alleviate or allow suffering to continue.[5] For many, such entrance, such seeing, is simply too difficult. Soelle acknowledges this when she refers to her own growing awareness of the danger of nuclear destruction. She did not want to see, she says; she did not want to hear or to understand what she was hearing.[6]

Such denial can also take place within healthcare itself. It may manifest itself in an insensitivity to the pain, a reduction of the person to a symptom or an illness, or a curtness with those who do not "try to get better." The words of one physician speak of the burden of sharing others' suffering. "There is only so much you can tolerate—all the problems, the calls, all the patients and families. I didn't bargain for this when I went into private practice. I had no idea it would be so hard. By the end of the week I feel I can barely stand it anymore."[7]

Sometimes, others' pain seems too much to bear. To deny our own suffering and the suffering of others is an understandable response. It is also an ineffective one. Suffering will not go away because we wish it to.

RESISTANCE

Suffering can enrage us. It can fill us with anger and lead us to fight against it with all our strength. Suffering sometimes becomes personalized; it is the enemy that we must fight and overcome. This response manifests itself in our culture's propensity to reach for a pill at the first sign of pain. It also manifests itself in the tireless dedication of scientists and researchers who have struggled to find cures for diseases and learn how to control pain. Resistance to unbearable suffering, our own or others', ultimately leads us to act. Such resistance is the essence of revolution, of the tearing down of walls. Resistance is a healthier response to suffering than denial; resistance recognizes the reality of affliction and moves to alleviate. At the same time, resistance poses a danger. Suffering itself can become the enemy, and the suffering person, the one whose intactness is threatened, is lost in the struggle.

ACCEPTANCE

Finally, some counsel acceptance of suffering. There is a very realistic basis for this response. Acceptance neither seeks to deny human experience nor supposes that it can overcome what ultimately cannot be overcome. Suffering, both personal and communal, exists. It is a fundamental aspect of the mystery of human existence. When one accepts suffering and dares to enter into its heart looking for meaning, one often discovers wisdom and depths of courage that amaze us. Some persons' suffering makes them appear to us as "gold that has been refined in the fire" (Wis 3:6). Accepted suffering ennobles and transforms. People find strength and sensitivity they never knew they had. Hagar, in Margaret Laurence's *The Stone Angel,* is such a person. Ninety years old, Hagar is a thoroughly unpleasant woman, totally insensitive and consistently critical. She finds herself in a hospital, in great pain. In her pain, Hagar slowly begins to recognize the pain of others and comes to accept the care of others, even of the son whom she has always rejected. One evening, Hagar gets out of bed and is found by a nurse.

> S he leads me back to bed. Then she does something else, and at first I don't understand.
>
> "It's like a little bed-jacket, really. It's nothing. It's just to keep you from harm. It's for your own protection."
>
> Coarse linen, it feels like. She slides my arms in and ties the harness firmly to the bed. I pull, and find I'm knotted and held like a trussed fowl.
>
> "I won't have this. I won't stand for it. It's not right. Oh, it's mean—"
>
> The nurse's voice is low, as though she were half ashamed of what she'd done. "I'm sorry. But you might fall, you see, and—"
>
> "Do you think I'm crazy, that I have to be put into this rig?"
>
> "Of course not. You might hurt yourself, that's all. Please—"
>
> I hear the desperation in her voice. Now that I think of it, what else can she do? She can't sit here by my bed all night.
>
> "I have to do it," she says. "Don't be angry."
>
> She has to do it. Quite right. It's not her fault. Even I can see that.
>
> "All right." I can barely hear my own voice, but I hear her slight answering sigh.
>
> "I'm sorry," she says helplessly, apologizing needlessly, perhaps on behalf of God, who never apologizes.
>
> Then I'm the one who's sorry.
>
> "I've caused you so much trouble..."[8]

Hagar's suffering leads her to recognize the problems others have, to "hear the desperation" in another's voice. It also allows her, for the first time in her life, to say she is sorry. Suffering, when accepted and dealt with, can transform us.

Acceptance as a response to suffering, although realistic and potentially transformative, can also be dangerous. Passive acceptance can diminish people, encourage them to give up on life and on themselves. To urge others to accept their sufferings can sometimes be our own way of denying reality and refusing compassion. "What do I do with all of this suffering?"

RESOURCES FROM OUR TRADITION

The Catholic healthcare ministry is holy work that takes place on holy ground. It is a blessed, sacramental ministry that reveals the compassionate presence of God in our world. It is also a very difficult ministry, and the holy ground often seems to be a lonely desert. Suffering, with all of its intensity, complexity, and mystery, is the landscape of the desert. What food, what beauty, what hope can we find? What can our tradition offer us for sustenance in the face of all this suffering? Can the Judaic-Christian tradition help us in our response to suffering?

The Judaic-Christian tradition comes out of human experience and the encounter with the divine that occurs in human experience. This tradition seeks to articulate what it has recognized as revelation and strives to allow that revelation to interpret life. Just as the question of suffering is basic to human life, it is also basic to any faith tradition, including the Judaic-Christian. The tradition recognizes that, ultimately, life is mystery and that no one can ever fully articulate, explain, or codify the human experience. At the same time, it recognizes that suffering is an essential aspect of that mystery. The account of "The Fall" in Chapter Three of Genesis is an attempt to deal with the questions of suffering and death. The authors of this text, recognizing the frailty of their own lives and their own people, relate that frailty to an original refusal of God's word. They attempt to show that human beings have consistently disfigured the image in which they were created. The accounts of creation and of The Fall remind us of human imperfection and of the constant need for God's merciful intervention. They do not, however, really explain suffering.

The classic attempt at explanation is to be found in the book of Job. Although Job and his family and his friends try to resolve the mystery, they never fully succeed, and Job ultimately bows before the God whom he has seen (Job 42:1-6).[9]

Although the tradition cannot offer us a ready explanation or a simple solution to the problem of suffering, it can offer us sustenance in suffering and direction in our response to it. Many sources and images address suffering, but four of these are particularly significant within the Catholic healthcare ministry: the image of God, the compassion of God, the covenant with God, and lamentation.

THE IMAGE OF GOD

The first account of creation in Genesis (Gen 1:1-2:3) provides us with one of our most fundamental definitions of the human person: "in the image of God God created them; male and female God created them. And God blessed them" (Gen 1:27-28). Women and men are those who have been created in the image of God. We often remark that a child is the image of the parent. When we say this, we mean that the adult's traits, appearances, and characteristics are revealed in the child. To look at the child is somehow to see the parent. To look at those created in God's image is to behold a reflection of the divine. Human beings have the potential to be the revelation of the divine in this world. As such, they possess a value and a dignity that is undeniable and that must never be disregarded. This fact has significant ramifications in terms of human suffering.

First, the dignity of the human person is a powerful call to alleviate suffering. Suffering often diminishes people, weakens them, and isolates them from each other. Reverence for the human person demands that we seek to enhance the person and struggle against what diminishes and disfigures the image.

Second, this same reverence speaks to the quality of our service. The sufferings of others can never be taken lightly; no human cry of pain can be disregarded. Although the temptation to turn away is strong, although the tendency to deny quickly comes to us, we are obligated to see, respect, and preserve the dignity of each person, especially those whose dignity is in jeopardy. For those who care for persons suffering and in pain, this reality calls us to sensitivity and tenderness in our care, since we care for what is most precious.

That persons who suffer bear God's image is very significant. Physical disfigurement and mental impairment do not destroy the image that we are. Divine radiance often shines through human frailty. Despite the ravages of illness, one still has the potential to reveal God's presence to others. May reminds us of this in a poignant article concerning Dax Cowart, a young man horribly burned. After years of struggle, even after he struggled to die, Cowart is still alive. He has made a meaningful life for himself. May says that even though he is terribly disfigured, Cowart lives now as a transformed human being. When one meets him, one finds "more than a patient encased and obscured by the surgeon's art ... the uncanny radiance of a man."[10] In the uncanny radiance of any person, one finds glimpses of the divine.

The belief that we are made in the image of God calls all who serve to revere God's image and preserve the person's dignity.

THE COMPASSION OF GOD

We have seen that the biblical understanding of God always involves compassion. God is recognized as the one who "is near to the broken hearted, and saves the crushed in spirit" (Ps 34:18). God's compassion is made visible in Jesus. His tender, sensitive healing activity leaves us with no doubt that God reaches out to save those who suffer.

Another aspect to God's compassion, however, is rich in meaning in the face of suffering. "Com-passion" is more than sympathy or pity; it is "feeling-with" another, sharing in her or his experience. The great Jewish scholar, Abraham Joshua Heschel, has shown the extent of God's com-passion. In his work, *The Prophets,* Heschel shows that the vocation (and the anguish) of the prophets is that they not only speak for God but also *feel* for God. The prophets carry the burden of experiencing what happens in God's heart. The reason for prophecy, according to Heschel, is God's involvement in the world. The biblical view of God holds that God can be affected by the activity of humankind, that human deeds can move God, can gladden, please, or grieve God. Heschel describes this involvement as the *pathos* of God. He compares the God of the philosophers with the God of Israel.

> The God of the philosophers is like the Greek *ananke,* unknown and indifferent to man; He thinks, but does not speak; He is conscious of Himself, but oblivious of the world; while the God of Israel is a God who loves, a God Who is known to, and concerned with, humankind. God not only rules the world in the majesty of God's might and wisdom, but reacts intimately to the events of history. God does not judge one's deeds impassively and with aloofness; God's judgment is imbued with the attitude of the One to Whom those actions are of the most intimate and profound concern. God does not stand outside the range of human suffering and sorrow. God is personally involved in, even stirred by, the conduct and fate of humankind.
>
> Pathos denotes, not an idea of goodness, but a living care; not an immutable example, but an outgoing challenge, a dynamic relation between God and humanity; not mere feeling or passive affection, but an act or attitude composed of various spiritual elements; no mere contemplative survey of the world, but a passionate summons.[11]

Heschel reminds us that the biblical tradition reveals to us a God who is present, who weeps when we weep, and who "does not stand outside the range of human suffering and sorrow." We have seen that God is present in human experience. Nowhere is that presence more surprising and more vital than in our suffering. God is present in the midst of our anguish, but not as a judge meting out punishment, or as a detached observer. The divine is present as *care,* as the One who knows what we suffer and who shares in our affliction. Even when this same God seems absent, faith summons us to attention, to openness, and to grace.

Jesus, the incarnation of the one God, manifests God's pathos. He did not stand outside of human suffering but entered into its very depths; he was made perfect through his sufferings (Heb 2:10). The gospels tell us that Jesus knew intense suffering and knew it in all its aspects. He experienced excruciating physical pain, pain unto death. He also knew the terrible isolation that suffering brings. We are shown a person who is alone in prayer to God, alone before his accusers, and terribly alone in his death. "My God, why have you abandoned me?" (Mt 27:46). Betrayed by one he has called friend, abandoned by those who promise never to leave him, Jesus reveals how intense is God's involvement in human existence. There is nothing from which God remains aloof. When human beings suffer, therefore, they never do so alone.

The Pauline epistles provide us with an interpretation of the meaning of Jesus' suffering. They tell us that suffering can be redemptive. Paul frequently uses the phrase "for us." In his letter to the Christians in Rome, for example, he writes: "While we were still weak, at the right time Christ died for the ungodly. Why, one will hardly die for a righteous person—though perhaps for a good person one will dare even to die. But God shows his love for us in that while we were yet sinners Christ died for us" (Rom 5:6-8).[12]

Paul writes to the early communities and consistently reminds them that Jesus suffered and died "for us." By this he means that Jesus' suffering and death were not simply social or political acts. Jesus endured suffering that God might bring about the salvation of humankind. He embraced the worst that life can offer us so that *all* life might be held in God's saving love. The book of Isaiah promised this when it spoke of the one who would bear our stripes, through whom we would be healed (Is 53:4-5). Jesus suffered that we might be healed; he cried out in anguish that our cries might be answered. This is the great realization of early Christianity: the one whom Isaiah had promised appeared in Jesus and acted on the behalf of all.

Paul also recognized that, just as Jesus had shared the fate of humankind, we now share the fate of Jesus. Believers share in the life and death of Jesus Christ. Joined to him as a branch is grafted onto a tree (Rom 11:17-24), our sufferings are his. The baptized have died with Christ; they now walk with him, and they shall rise with him (Rom 6:4-5).

In the light of faith, suffering takes on meaning. Joined with Jesus' suffering, it is redeemed. The Judaic-Christian tradition tells us that the divine is present to and transforms human suffering. God's pathos, made flesh in Jesus Christ, is involved in suffering, and is present to the one who suffers.

It is important to remember that, even as suffering can be redemptive, it remains a mystery. God's presence in human suffering is neither an invitation to accept pain passively, nor an excuse for the unconscionable suffering that humans inflict on each other. The passionate summons that Heschel speaks of is answered in every act we make to combat suffering that rises from oppression, violence, and sin. Each time a healthcare giver acts with compassion and dares to enter into another's pain, God's pathos is again present in our world.

THE COVENANT WITH GOD

The faith tradition in which the Catholic healthcare ministry finds its home trusts in God's ongoing presence because it has a heritage of covenant. A major theme in both the Hebrew and the Christian scriptures is that of covenant. Covenant is the bond established between God and the people; it is a relationship of mutual belonging. The book of Exodus tells us that God brought the people out of slavery into the desert on their way to a promised land. When the people came to Mount Sinai, God established covenant with them. "You shall be my people and I shall be your God" (see Ex 19:4-6; Deut 7:6-9). Chosen by God among all the peoples of the earth, God's people are given the opportunity to respond to God's initiative. If they enter into covenant, they will belong to God and God will belong to them.

To say that God belongs to the people does not mean that the people own or possess God, but rather that God has chosen to enter into a relationship that becomes progressively more intimate. God will never abandon the people. God's presence, seen in fire and thunder, spoken from a mountaintop, ultimately comes to dwell among the people in the person of a son. Although the people rebel and sin, God remains faithful to covenant and does not desert them. The biblical texts reflect a strong conviction that *God has acted in Israel's history* and that God continues to act. Covenant is more than a legal agreement; it is profound and constant commitment of both parties. The people, for their part, will live in such a way as to manifest that they are indeed the people of God. They will keep the law, not because the law will make them holy, but because the way of the law is how one lives if one belongs to God. They also will care for each other.

Covenant with God necessarily implies covenant among the people themselves. Belonging to God, the people belong to each other. They must care for each other, comfort each other, and make sure that the fragile ones among them are protected. Covenant established that those in the desert were not a group of individuals with each making his or her own way to a promised land. They may have begun the journey that way, but covenant made them a people responsible for each other.

Although the Church may not use the term "covenant" very frequently today, it remains conscious of its identity as a people responsible for each other. The most well-known expression of that consciousness is the often-cited beginning of the "Pastoral Constitution on the Church in the Modern World" issued at Vatican II: "The joys and the hopes, the griefs and the anxieties of the men and women of this age, especially those who are poor or in any way afflicted, these too are the joys and hopes, the griefs and anxieties of the followers of Christ."[13] The reality of covenant, therefore, grounds our trust in God's presence in the midst of suffering.

Covenant also calls us as healthcare givers. It is a manifestation of the passionate summons that Heschel emphasizes. Covenant calls us to care for those who suffer. We belong to and are responsible for each other. When we risk entering into the suffering of others and stay with them, we are true to our identity as people of the covenant.

> When I was a young man, I worked as a student health physician in L.A. A young Jewish woman came to see me; and after an initial examination, it was apparent that she had a fatal disease. When I informed her, she broke down. She was about to be married. How was she going to tell her fiance? What was she going to do? I told her I would be happy to do whatever I could. So I sat down with the two of them as they struggled with their decision. They eventually decided to get married. I remember how happy they were. She followed me into private practice and I treated her for the next four years. When she died, I cried. I still hear from her husband. Every Christmas he sends me a card with pictures of his four children and his new wife. They felt they had a gift to give to each other and I felt part of it.[14]

This is a story of covenant people. A physician enters into the pain of a young woman. A fiance also enters, even though it will cause him pain as well. Together, the three know sorrow and they know happiness, part of a gift to give each other.

LAMENTATION

One of the most terrible effects of pain and affliction is the loss of language. Pain is difficult to describe; suffering often renders one mute. "There are forms of suffering that reduce one to a silence in which no discourse is possible any longer, in which a person ceases reacting as a human agent," says Soelle.[15] Scarry states this even more strongly: "Physical pain does not simply resist language, but actively destroys it, bringing about an immediate reversion to a state anterior to language, to the sounds and cries a human being makes before language is learned."[16] The tendency of suffering to rob us of language is enhanced by our culture's emphasis on suffering in silence, on keeping "a stiff upper lip." Such silence serves to further isolate and alienate those who suffer. They cannot speak their pain; they cannot communicate their anguish. They cannot speak their fear or their anger, especially at God.

The Judaic-Christian tradition provides important sustenance in the face of such silence. We have a heritage of lamentation. The lament is the voice of grief. It cries out and gives voice to pain. The prophet Jeremiah lamented not only the sin of Israel but also his own fate. He did not choose to be a prophet and cries against the God who has called him. Jeremiah speaks for all who suffer when he shouts, "Cursed be the day on which I was born! The day when my mother bore me, let it not be blessed. Why did I come forth from the womb to see toil and sorrow, and spend my days in shame?" (Jer 20:14, 18). Jeremiah's lament reminds us that God's followers have never been afraid to voice their pain, have never hidden their anguish from their God.

The Psalms, voice of Israel at worship and prayer of the Church, are filled with lamentation (Pss 16, 22, 73, 88, 116 are good examples). Both individuals and the people collectively describe their pain; they demand that God come to their aid. Psalms of lament "express the pain, grief, dismay, and anger that life is not good. (They also refuse to settle for things as they are, and so they assert hope.)"[17] The Psalms themselves are rich sustenance for those who cannot find their own words. They enable the suffering to join with generations of those whose anguish has found voice. They also tell us that suffering in silence and denying our rage are not necessary. Ours is a tradition that dares to be honest before its God, that knows our God will hear and respond. There is food for our journey even in the deepest of deserts.

A tour of any healthcare facility leads us to wonderful places of healing. It also takes us into suffering that seems too much to bear. Nothing will make suffering disappear, but a tradition lives in people who know they are God's image, who experience and give compassion, who take covenant seriously, and who are able to speak and be heard. This tradition helps us as we ask: "What shall I do with all of this suffering?"

Notes

1. Eric J. Cassel, "The Nature of Suffering and the Goals of Medicine," *The New England Journal of Medicine,* March 18, 1982, p. 640.
2. Cassel, p. 643.
3. Simone Weil, "The Love of God and Affliction," *Waiting for God,* trans. by E. Crawford, G. P. Putnam's Sons, New York, 1951, p. 117.
4. Richard F. Vieth lists 12 possible theological responses to suffering in *Holy Power, Human Pain,* Meyer Stone Books, Bloomington, IN, 1988, p. 25.
5. Dorothee Soelle, *Suffering,* trans. by E. R. Kalin, Fortress Press, Philadelphia, 1975, p. 32.
6. Dorothee Soelle, excerpts from a speech given in Amsterdam, 1981. Reprinted in Cambridge Women's Peace Collective, *My Country Is the Whole World,* Pandora Press, London, 1984, p. 231.
7. Arthur Kleinman, *The Illness Narratives: Suffering, Healing and the Human Condition,* Basic Books, Inc., New York, 1988, p. 214.
8. Margaret Laurence, *The Stone Angel,* Seal Books, Toronto, 1964, p. 255.
9. Walter Burghardt makes this point in his article, "Is Being 'Catholic' Worth Saving?" *Health Progress,* September, 1985, 107-114, p. 111.
10. William F. May, "A 'New Phoenix'? Reflections on the Dax Burn Case," *Bulletin of the Park Ridge Center,* July/August 1988, p. 4.
11. Abraham Joshua Heschel, *The Prophets,* Harper & Row Torchbooks, New York, 1969, vol. 2, p. 4.
12. See also Rom 8:27-34; 1 Cor 1:13, 15:3; Gal 1:4.
13. "Pastoral Constitution on the Church in the Modern World," No. 1 in Walter Abbott, ed., *The Documents of Vatican II,* New Century Books, Piscataway, NJ, 1966, p. 199.
14. *The Dynamics of Catholic Identity in Healthcare: A Working Document,* Catholic Health Association, St. Louis, 1987, p. 39.
15. Soelle, *Suffering,* p. 68.
16. Elaine Scarry, *The Body in Pain: The Making and Unmaking of the World,* Oxford University Press, Oxford, NY, 1985, p. 4.
17. Walter Brueggemann, *Praying the Psalms,* St. Mary's Press, Winona, MN, 1986, p. 29.

5

"Will Everything Be Okay?"

DEATH AND DYING IN THE JUDAIC-CHRISTIAN TRADITION

People who experience hospice care for the first time are often surprised at the sense of peace they find. Death seems to come quietly and with a certain deference. Dying persons, and their loved ones, are cared for in dignity and compassion. The dying are helped to know: "You matter to the last moment of your life, and we will do all we can not only to help you die peacefully, but to live until you die."[1]

Emergency rooms and trauma centers present another picture of death. They remind us that death can be violent, brutal, and senseless. The head nurse of an inner-city hospital emergency room tells of such a death.

> A young woman used to come in here a lot. She had five kids and no husband. She used to bring the kids in when something happened to one of them. We got to know her and the kids pretty well. The oldest was about 12 years old, and he used to take care of the younger ones—kind of shepherd them around. She was a good woman and tried to raise her kids with some religion, some values. One night she was shot. They brought her and the kids in here. She died. We gave the kids some time alone with her. When they came out, the oldest one was carrying the youngest one. He looked at me and said, "If we go to church now, will everything be okay?"

The pain of death, its incomprehensible finality, can often leave us speechless. What can one say to a young boy whose mother has been brutally killed, who has been left alone with four younger siblings? What can one say to a nurse who stands helpless in the face of such anguish? Death frequently defies our understanding; it defies what is basic to the human person: our will to live. Death can rob us, take from us those whom we love and whose lives give meaning to our own. For the healthcare giver, whose desire is to alleviate suffering and preserve life, death can often be experienced as a terrible, personal defeat.

Death is an absolute. No one can avoid it; no one can control it. We can, however, try to find its meaning and struggle to give voice to our own coping with death. If suffering is mystery, even more so is death. If the meaning we give to suffering influences how we deal with it, even more so with death. Since death is the absolute, how we regard it largely determines how we regard life itself. We all know this instinctively, but we often fail to make this knowledge explicit. Sometimes wisdom about death comes to us from unexpected sources.

The Washington Post featured a rather unusual article in its sports section. The article discussed the trials and tribulations of the new head coach of the University of Alabama football team. It seems that many of Alabama's fiercely loyal fans were not pleased with his performance and made their displeasure known. The coach, however, was not overly concerned; he was able to place his present problems in a larger perspective. He had, he said, a "good theology of death." He went on to say, "If you don't have a good theology of death, you will not have a good theology of life. Period. Once having dealt with (death), there's not much that scares you."[2] The meaning this football coach had given to death enabled him to live his life with courage and peace.

MEANINGS OF DEATH

As with suffering, everyone must ascribe her or his own meaning to death. There are, however, many common approaches. Some will agree with a Dylan Thomas, who rages against the "dark night" that is death.[3] Others see death as the end, with nothing to follow. Some regard death as a release from unbearable pain or agonizing sorrow. Still others view death as transformation, as movement into a new mode of being. Many faith traditions hold that death is mystery, that although it is inescapable, it is not ultimately victorious. A theology of death influences life; death's meaning shapes response to death's reality.

RESPONSES TO DEATH

Although each person gives meaning (or non-meaning) to death and each thus responds to it in a uniquely personal way, the three responses to suffering explored in Chapter 4 are also the most common responses to death. As a culture, we deny death, we resist it, or we seek to accept it. Elisabeth Kubler-Ross would say that most people do all three at different moments in their encounter with death. She is undoubtedly correct.[4] In the fabric of our society, however, denial, resistance, and acceptance have each taken on lives of their own.

DENIAL

"The idea of death, the fear of it, haunts the human animal like nothing else; it is a mainspring of human activity—activity designed largely to avoid the fatality of death, to overcome it by denying in some way that it is the final destiny for the human person."[5] "Americans like to appear as if they give death hardly any thought at all. Of course, death will happen to all of us someday, but until then, it is not something to think about or grapple with."[6] These two quotations address a strong instinct in our culture. We do not want to grapple with death. We wish to pretend that it doesn't really happen, at least not to us.

One of the most common ways in which death is denied is in our fascination with and exaltation of youth. We see commercials and advertisements that promise us youthful skin, young bodies, and flowing blond hair. Everywhere we look, youth is hoped for and promised. Although the aging persons of our society have done much to enhance the image of the older American, they have most often done so by stressing how *young* older Americans really are. If we can just stay young, death will remain in the background.

Denial of death, especially the power of death, can be a subtle factor in our approach to healthcare. Healthcare givers, reluctant to acknowledge the finality of death, sometimes distance themselves from dying patients. One woman recounts her experience when her father was dying.

> I recall sadly the change in the attitude of my father's personal physician, a man of his own age, during my father's last stay in the hospital. With the worsening of my father's condition, the physician stopped being friendly and warm; his visits became rare and brief; his manner became quite detached, almost angry. I understand now that the process of death can

release overwhelming emotions not only in patients but also in physicians. Physicians may not be prepared to handle the situation either as physicians or as bystanders.[7]

It is natural for human beings to want to deny death, to spend great energy in doing so. The specter of death reminds us that ultimately everyone must give over that power so important to all people: control over their own lives. Denial of death is also denial of the powerlessness of the individual who faces death and of the caregiver who cannot prevent that death from occurring. All such denial is fruitless, however, because every human person will die.

RESISTANCE

Frederick Wiseman's PBS documentary, *Near Death,* presents a thought-provoking study of life in an intensive care unit of a large hospital. It follows the lives of four families who must face the death of a loved one. One woman faces the prospect of losing her beloved husband, Charlie. When asked about any orders for her husband's treatment her immediate response is that "everything must be done." She cannot bear to lose her Charlie, and no possible treatment or intervention must be denied him.

Her response is one of love. "He's my life!" she says. We cannot easily let go of those we love. We resist death even more strongly than we resist suffering. Such resistance is often heroic. It has resulted in life-saving discoveries, the elimination of many diseases, and the prolongation of life expectancy. Resistance to the death of others springs from compassion and reverence for human life. Resistance to our own death springs from that same reverence and from our sense that life is to be cherished.

The struggle against death is valid and should not be abandoned. At the same time, resistance can become problematic. Death can become a personal enemy. Persons can be made to endure excruciating suffering to stave off a death that is certain to come anyway. The question must always be asked: Are we prolonging life—or death?

ACCEPTANCE

I walked into her hospital room. She was seated in a chair. She looked lovely and truly gracious. I didn't know her well at all. We talked about her diagnosis and her treatment. "I don't want a lot of chemotherapy or any desperate measures. I've had a long full life and I'm not afraid. In fact, I am curious and curiously peaceful. I have spent my life searching for God and I want to finally see him." I was a brand new Provincial Superior, she a nun for over fifty years. She gave me courage and hope. She had lived through great changes and always said to me, "God has been with us this far, God will continue to be with us. I don't worry about the future of the congregation." She never lost faith. She had her sense of humor to the very last moment. She died on the fourth of July.

This "curiously peaceful" woman shows us how death can be accepted. For her, death was not an absolute end but rather a passage to full vision. For some people, acceptance of death endows them with a dignity and a perspective that they never lose. To accept the reality of death enables one to say that "there's not much else that scares you." To accept the death of loved ones enables us to be with them in their dying, to let them go in love. Charlie's wife gradually came to realize that her husband would not get better. She changed her request that everything be done for her husband to one for comfort and relief of pain.

Acceptance of death enables many people to live their last moments in dignity and peace. Some deaths, however, cannot be easily accepted. A young mother, killed in violence, who suddenly leaves five young children alone—this cannot and should not be accepted with equanimity. Any of the deaths we human beings inflict on each other also should not be accepted. Further some people can never accept death. The fear is so great, death so unknown, that they cannot go gently, but "rage against the night."[8] There is no "perfect" way to die, no "best" way to accept what is always mystery.

Denial, resistance, acceptance—all these are part of humanity's confrontation with death. None of these "solves" the problem of death; none enables us to manage it completely. Death remains the great mystery and the great sorrow of human existence. Even in the face of death, however, faith takes courage, and our tradition finds meaning and hope.

DEATH IN THE LIGHT OF FAITH

Theology seeks to bring the light of faith to bear on the complexities of human existence. Nowhere is that light more needed than in the darkness of death. How do people of faith understand death, how do they respond to it? Is there, even here, food for the journey? "Will everything be okay?" All that we have seen of human beings made in the image of God, the compassion of God, our reality as people of covenant, and the tradition of lamentation in terms of suffering are also important in terms of death. We are God's image even in death; our sacredness is not lost. Our God's presence and amazing compassion goes with us even into death. Because we are a people who belong to God and to each other, we share in sorrow; we do not abandon even as we are not abandoned. Just as we can voice our suffering and cry out to our God in pain, we can voice the anguish of the fear and loss of death. There is further light, however, when we struggle with death itself. Faith promises us company on our journey; it gives us hope and calls us to courage.

COMPANY

One day I received a telephone call. "Please come to the hospital immediately. My sister has just been diagnosed with terminal cancer." I went to be with both women. The older sister was the strong one. She had always been the one to make the important decisions, to encourage her younger sister. The younger one had always found life to be difficult. She had spent years in counselling and was afraid of many, many things. Yet, *she* was the one with cancer. Her illness was a long and difficult one. She never did become reconciled to dying, no matter how much everyone— especially her sister—tried to encourage and comfort her. She died afraid. The older sister endured the anguish of watching her sister suffer. She was desolate because she could not take away the suffering. "If only I could die in her place. It would be so much easier for me!" But she could not.

Death is a terribly solitary thing. Each person dies alone. This is a source of anguish and loneliness for those who care for the dying. It is also frightening for the one who must die. No one can ever *really* know what death is, except the one who dies. There is one, however, who does know what it is to die, and to die alone. There is one who is able to go into our death with us.

Scripture scholars agree on very few things. They do agree, however, that the gospels as we have them today began with the accounts of Jesus' passion and death. These were the first memories collected, the first "blocks of material" joined together in the community's memory. Further, the passion accounts (Mt 26:1-27:66; Mk 14:1-15:47; Lk 22:1-23:56; Jn 18:1-19:42) occupy the proportionally largest section of the gospels. The story of Jesus' suffering and death was vital to the life of the early communities.

There is no question that Jesus died. It is how he died and why he died that concern us here. Jesus died in misery, anguish, and scandal.[9] He was condemned by both the religious leaders and the political rulers. He was beaten and mocked, and the manner of his death was that reserved for criminals and traitors. His death fulfilled the edict: "Cursed be he who hangs upon a tree" (Dt 21:23). His crucifixion took place outside the city walls so that Jerusalem would not be contaminated by such an ignominious death. Jesus knew the physical pain of beating, the shame of being stripped and held up to ridicule, the anguish of death, and he knew all this alone.

Two scenes in the passion story emphasize Jesus' solitude. In the first, Jesus' prayer in the garden at Gethsemane (Mk 14:32-42; Mt 26:36-46; Lk 22:40-46), Jesus takes his disciples with him to pray. He asks them to keep watch with him. In all three accounts, the disciples fall asleep. Those closest to Jesus, to whom he has just entrusted the words and actions of Eucharist, fall asleep and leave him alone to accept his death. There is no older sister who grieves that she cannot suffer another's death in this scene. The Master is alone before the God whom he calls "Abba," even as he struggles to accept what lies before him.

Later in the story, we behold Jesus as he stands bound and humiliated before the people of Jerusalem. He stands alone. He hears his own people cry, "Crucify him!" No voice is raised in defense of this person who has only done good. No attempt is made to rescue one who has been healer, friend, and bringer of good news. Jesus' passion and death tell us of a good, compassionate person who did not desire death but who accepted it and experienced it in all its anguish and torment. The passion account is a story of a loving person who asks only that his friends love each other and who is abandoned by those very friends. Here is someone who knows what it means to die, who evades not a second of suffering, and who understands the terrible loneliness of death.

Jesus' death tells us that there is nowhere that God is not present, even in death. Jesus Christ, Son of God, entered fully into humanity and shared all of it, its wonders and its anguish. He brought all this to the cross. He died, as he lived, "for us." His death transforms ours and promises us that even in the most solitary moment of our lives, we are not alone. There is one who knows, who lives now, who accompanies us. Nothing, not even death, can "separate us from the love of God in Christ Jesus our Lord" (Rom 8:37-39). Our cries of pain, anguish, and death are joined with those of God's Spirit, "who intercedes for us with sighs too deep for words" (Rom 8:26).

HOPE

Hope is a strange thing. It often seems absurd, and yet it stubbornly persists. It appears in unlikely places. The joy of life is often felt most intensely when it risks being lost. Etty Hillesum is a remarkable witness to such hope. Her diaries, written in the two years before her death at Auschwitz, reveal a luminous hope in the face of annihilation. She knew God was present to her and rejoiced in that presence.

> But I accept everything from your hands, oh God. But I still suffer from the same old complaint. I cannot stop searching for the great redeeming formula. For the one word that sums up everything within me, the overflowing and rich sense of life. "Why did You not make me a poet, oh God? But perhaps You did, and so I shall wait patiently until the words have grown inside me, the words that proclaim how good and beautiful it is to live in your world, oh God, despite everything we human beings do to one another."[10]

Early Christianity is marked by hope, unreasonable hope. A small band of people whose leader has been put to death in shame think they have encountered and been transformed by the Savior of the world. Further, they think they can transform the world. They endure suffering and ridicule, and they have no power. Still, however, as with Etty centuries later, they continue in joy and praise.

Hope must have some basis in reality, or it is not hope but rather delusion. Hope must also cling to a promised future; otherwise it becomes naive optimism. The reality of Christian hope rests in the resurrection of Jesus Christ. In the earliest statement of the Christian creed, Paul writes: "For I delivered to you as of first importance what I also received, that Christ died for our sins in accordance with the scriptures, that he was buried, that he was raised on the third day in accordance with the scriptures, and that he appeared to Cephas, then to the twelve" (1 Cor 15:3-5).

Christianity exists because it believes in the resurrection of Jesus Christ. In raising Jesus from the dead, God has shown a power that is stronger even than death. In the resurrection, human existence is transformed; death is not the end, life is. The risen Christ shows us that sin has been overcome, that suffering and death have been redeemed. The promise of creation has been fulfilled: God has saved the people. "If Christ has not been raised your faith is futile and you are still in your sins. ... But in fact Christ has been raised from the dead, the first fruits of those who have fallen asleep" (1 Cor 15:17, 20). Belief in the resurrection grounds hope, for Jesus' resurrection is God's statement that the fullness of life is our true destiny.

Hope posits a future; Jesus' resurrection shows us what that future will be. Paul tells us that Christ is the "first fruits of those who have fallen asleep." That is, what has happened to Jesus will happen to all of us. His fate is our fate. His fate is the fate of all creation.

> It (hope) sees in the resurrection of Christ not the eternity of heaven, but the future of the very earth on which his cross stands. It sees in him the future of the very humanity for which he died. That is why it finds the cross the hope of the earth. This hope struggles for the obedience of the body, because it awaits the quickening of the body. It espouses in all meekness the cause of the devastated earth and of harassed humanity, because it is promised possession of the earth. *Ave crux—unica spes!* (Hail the Cross — our singular hope)[11]

Thus, even in death, there is hope. In the midst of desolation, life triumphs. We have glimpsed God's power in Jesus' resurrection. We believe that power is also for us.

COURAGE

Etty Hillesum continued to hope in God even as she faced her and her family's death. Because of this, she was able to care for others, be a source of energy for them, and give them courage. A friend writes of the last time he saw her before she was taken to Auschwitz. She was standing on a platform, waiting to enter the train. "Talking gaily, smiling, a kind word for everyone she met on the way, full of sparkling humor, perhaps just a touch of sadness, but every inch the Etty you all know so well."[12]

Hope gives courage. The New Testament is eloquent witness to this. After the death of Jesus, the disciples were bewildered and afraid. After the resurrection, they were astonished and had difficulties believing. They gathered together in prayer, a small group of leaderless people. God sent the promised Spirit to these people, and they were transformed. They began to proclaim the good news and to move out to "the ends of the earth" with their message.

The early Christian communities experienced themselves as a people called by a God who had redeemed them. They believed that their future would be the one God had promised. Because of this, they acted with courage, even in the face of persecution and death.

The early Christians were not naive in their hope. They knew that they still lived in a world where death seemed to conquer. They recognized that death was the ultimate sign that sin still exercised power in the world. They did not expect that all their troubles would disappear, all their pain cease. They lived in the midst of suffering, and they did so with courage. Their courage enabled them to proclaim God's kingdom, continue to heal the sick, and drive out demons. It helped them to face difficulty and even death.

Courage is neither a painless reality nor one that knows no fear. Rather, courage dares to hold fast to hope. It dares to enter and endure present agony, confident that agony will ultimately be defeated. Courage for those who face death is an acceptance of what must be and a refusal to lose one's humanity in the process. Courage born of Christian hope holds fast to God's promise and looks to the cross as the ultimate witness that God saves in the depths of agony.

Courage born of hope sustains the healthcare giver. It invites one to dare to accompany the dying on their journey. It calls us to join in the grieving process, to not distance ourselves from those whom we feel we can no longer help. Rather than becoming brisk and distant, courage helps the physician (and all caregivers) to share in the dying person's own experience.

E very physician has a professional mandate to help other human beings in need. But the inevitability of a patient's death may challenge this code, unless the physician is willing to add a new dimension to the patient-doctor relationship: that of helping the patient deal with the experience of dying. Just as, over time, doctors have moved from dealing alone with the patient's disease to encouraging the patient's participation in the healing process, so they must begin to see how important it is for them to participate with the terminally ill patient in the process of death. The dying person needs to feel that he or she has not lost meaning for those who are close, one of whom is inevitably the doctor who has tried so hard to cure the patient.[13]

Ultimately, courage allows us to be helped by others. Many dying persons are a source of wisdom and grace. Their own courage increases ours. Their dignity speaks radiantly of the image of God that we all are. One who works in an AIDS hospice says this well:

It seems that with every dying patient I've treated, the burden of the future has been lifted from them. And in some ways, they're able to more readily focus on the present, and I can benefit from that. In many ways, dealing with people at this point in their lives is an incredible privilege.[14]

Courage, finally, is grace. Given to us in God's Spirit, anchored in belief in the resurrection, courage sustains us before what will remain mystery until the end of time.

"Will everything be okay?" Obviously not immediately. A twelve-year-old boy must still face the anguish of his mother's death, the burden of responsibilities too heavy for him to bear, and his family's probable disintegration. An older sister must still stand helpless before her younger sibling's fear of death. We all must eventually face our own deaths.

"Will everything be okay?" Ultimately, yes. We are a people of faith and of promise. In Jesus Christ, God has promised the resurrection of all, and we know God's promises are true. In the meantime, we live in courageous hope, daring to believe that the last word is not death but life. We hold tenaciously to the vision: "God will dwell with them, and they shall be God's people. God will wipe away every tear from their eyes, and death shall be no more, neither shall there be mourning nor crying nor pain any more, for the former things have passed away" (Rev 21:3-4).

"These words are trustworthy and true" (Rev 21:5).

Notes

1. From Dame Cecily Saunders, foundress of the modern hospice movement; quoted in William F. Carr, "Lead Me Safely Through Death," *America*, March 25, 1989, p. 265.
2. "Curry Bears the Pressure of Tide's Stormy Season," *The Washington Post*, Nov. 25, 1989, pp. CL, 4.
3. Dylan Thomas, "Do Not Go Gently into that Dark Night," *Collected Poems*, New Directions Paperbook, New York, 1971, p. 128.
4. Kubler-Ross' classic work, *On Death and Dying*, Macmillan Publishing Co., Inc., 1969, examines her well-known five stages of death and dying: denial and isolation, anger, bargaining, depression, and acceptance. See also Bonnie J. Miller-McLemore, "The Death and Dying Movement: Psychologies and the Formation of Culture, " *Second Opinion*, vol. 9, 1988, pp. 29-51.
5. Ernest Becker, *The Denial of Death*, New York, The Free Press, 1973, p. xi.
6. Arthur C. McGill, *Death and Life: An American Theology*, Fortress Press, Philadelphia, 1987, p. 13.
7. Egilde P. Seravalli, "The Dying Patient, the Physician, and the Fear of Death," *The New England Journal of Medicine*, Dec. 29, 1988, p. 1729.

8. Thomas, p. 128.

9. "Our religious language and imagery has made the cross a symbol of the sacred, of salvation, of the power of God, and we are too easily able to forget that behind the liturgical symbol lies a secular reality that is devastating in its meaning and its wider implications." Monika K. Hellwig, *Jesus the Compassion of God*, Michael Glazier, Inc., Wilmington, DE, 1983, p. 85.

10. *An Interrupted Life: The Diaries of Etty Hillesum 1941-43*, Washington Square Press, New York, 1983, p. 209.

11. Jurgen Moltmann, *Theology of Hope: On the Grounds and the Implications of a Christian Eschatology*, trans. by James W. Leight, SCM Press, London, 1967, p. 21.

12. *Interrupted Life*, p. 275.

13. Seravalli, p. 1729.

14. From Michael Clement; quoted in "Deathbed Medicine," *American Medical News*, July 7, 1989, p. 39.

6

"There's Something About the Gospel ..."

CATHOLIC SOCIAL TEACHING AND HEALTHCARE OF THE POOR

One evening, a group of healthcare professionals gathered together to reflect on "What keeps you going?" Members of the group were asked to recall an image that reminded them what they were doing was worthwhile. One member's image was that of a pot-bellied stove. When he became discouraged, he said, he remembered that stove. As the administrator of a rural hospital, he was also responsible for a clinic in a remote mountain setting.

Once a month we'd get into the van and drive up to that village. We'd set up our equipment in the local Legion Hall. We'd set out coffee and donuts, and we'd light the pot-bellied stove. By the time people started coming in, the stove had warmed the whole place. Everyone would gather around that stove—for warmth and for companionship. We would treat the people who needed us. We listened to their tales, diagnosed their illnesses, offered what help we could. We got to know a lot of the people in the area, shared their life stories. I think many people came to the clinic for the companionship as much as for the medicine. The pot-bellied stove symbolized it all for me. It warmed people, brought them together, helped them get better. I used to think, "This is what healthcare's all about."

Healthcare facilities never exist in isolation. Hospitals, clinics, psychiatric facilities, long-term care facilities ... all these exist in neighborhoods, areas characterized by types of people, buildings, schools, and industries (or lack thereof). Neighborhoods have unique flavors, specific noise levels, even their own languages. Sometimes the neighborhood is in a busy urban city, sometimes in a suburban setting, sometimes in a rural area. What happens in the neighborhood affects what happens in the healthcare facility, and what happens in the facility affects the neighborhood.

Changes in the neighborhood inevitably mean changes for the facility. People move away, the Legion Hall closes, the pot-bellied stove remains unlit. City neighborhoods change, and a thriving acute care hospital faces serious financial difficulties when more and more poor and uninsured seek help in its emergency room. On the other hand, an outreach program from the local healthcare facility reduces the infant mortality rate in the neighborhood and everyone benefits. The healthcare facility can never be isolated from the community of people in which it exists, since that community is a major reason for its existence.

The same is true of the Church. It cannot live in isolation from its neighborhood. This fact was recognized by the earliest of Christian communities. The Gospel of Luke concludes, and the Acts of the Apostles begins, with a statement by Jesus that the disciples were to be his witnesses from Jerusalem to the ends of the earth (Lk 24:46-48; Acts 1:8). After Pentecost and the gift of the Holy Spirit, Jesus' disciples immediately left the seclusion of their room of prayer and went out into the streets. Their story is one of travel, proclamation, and healing. From a very small beginning in the local villages, Christianity rapidly spread and grew.

> In the early decades of the Roman Empire, a new sect of Judaism appeared and spread rapidly, though not in great numbers, through the cities of the East. It did not stand out among the many "Oriental" cults being carried from place to place by immigrants and traders. Few people of importance paid attention to it. Its origins were unnoticed by writers of the day. Yet it was to become a new religion, separate from, … the Jewish communities that gave it birth. In a few centuries it would become not only the dominant religion of the Roman Empire'but unique in its imperial sponsorship.[1]

Although Christianity's involvement in the world of its time might seem natural to us today, this was not necessarily the case. Christians had in their midst another model of living according to belief, the community of believers at Qumran. Qumran is the name of an area near Jericho where archeologists discovered many texts (the "Dead Sea Scrolls") and subsequently uncovered the ruins of a developed community of people who lived there from approximately 135-110 BC until 68 AD. This community was religiously based and originated in protest to the infidelities of Jewish religious leadership. Their lives were based on the demands of the Hebrew scriptures, and they waited anxiously for the Messiah's arrival.[2]

Christians, too, had awaited the Messiah's arrival and lived from the Hebrew scriptures. They differed from their counterparts in two very important ways. First, their experience of the risen Christ convinced them that the Messiah had indeed come. Second, this same experience convinced them that they belonged in the world. They did not retreat to a remote area and build their own world. They were not content to critique the world from a distance. They chose rather to transform it from within. Something in the Christian message and in Christian life calls for the transformation of the world. The Gospel is good news, meant to be proclaimed. This cannot be done from a distance.

The Church has always recognized this fact, and throughout its history, it has spoken to the social conditions of its time. Sometimes it has done so with prophetic witness, sometimes with caution and less-than-heroic measures. The past century, however, has been marked by an unprecedented and steady flow of teachings of the official Catholic Church that address the social reality of the modern world. This body of teachings, known frequently as the Social Teachings of the Church, provides us with important and challenging perspectives on our relationship to our various "neighborhoods."

THE SOCIAL TEACHINGS OF THE CHURCH

I drove into the parking lot this morning, thinking about what I was going to do today. I wasn't paying attention to what was going on. I do this every day and it's just routine. I heard a lot of noise, I looked up and saw that the entrance to the lot was blocked—by picketers! I had to back up and try to find a place to park on the street. When I did, I got out of my car and tried to find out what was going on. It seems that people in the neighborhood were protesting because the hospital had purchased some property and had then let it deteriorate very badly. These people were really angry! They said that the vacant buildings were open invitations to drug dealers, that kids were getting mugged there, that the hospital had to do something—and now!

For the first time in a long time, I looked around me at the area in which I worked. It resembled a battle zone: broken windows, trash in the street, abandoned cars, groups standing on corners. It was a mess. I remembered how it was when I first came here. The neighborhood was a relatively quiet one, there were little diners and coffee shops we used to go to for lunch, people sometimes smiled on the streets. I had never even really noticed the change. I had never really thought about what it meant.

Very often, we do not notice change in our lives or our surroundings until someone starts shouting. Catholic social teaching is not usually a shout, but it is a strong, clear voice. This body of teaching includes the writings of various popes and bishops, the documents of Vatican Council II, the documents of international synods of bishops, and the writings of regional groupings (conferences) of bishops. Such works point out socioeconomic changes and what these do to people. The first such teaching is Pope Leo XIII's encyclical *Rerum Novarum* ("On the Condition of Labor"),[3] published in 1891. In this encyclical, Leo XIII sought to respond to the deplorable conditions of workers in his time. He brought the wisdom of Catholic tradition into dialogue with, and judgment on, the unjust working conditions that prevailed in the Western world at the end of the nineteenth century.

From the publication of *Rerum Novarum* until today, Church leaders have continued to address the socioeconomic reality in terms of basic Christian values and the Christian justice tradition. Schultheis, DeBerri, and Henriot list "twelve major lessons" that appear in the body of social teaching.

1. The documents stress that the social reality is not separated from the religious dimension of life; rather, it must be transformed in light of the Gospel.
2. The dignity of the human person is a constant theme in all the documents.
3. All human persons have inalienable rights which must be respected and protected by the institutions of society.
4. An emerging recognition of the growing gap between the rich and the poor leads to an insistence on a preferential option for the poor.
5. Love of neighbor, a demand of the Gospel, implies action for justice.
6. Promotion of the common good is of primary importance.
7. The principle of subsidiarity (responsibility and decision making at the level closest to local communities and institutions) should be respected.
8. The teachings encourage participation in the political processes of one's country as a means of achieving the common good.
9. Economic justice is vital, since the economy exists for the people's betterment.
10. The writings stress that the world's goods belong to all of the world's people, all must share the earth's resources.
11. The documents call for a global solidarity.
12. Social teachings also call for just peace among all men and women.[4]

Changing social realities as well as developing understandings have led to different emphases in the social teachings of the past century. The experience of global war, for example, generated significant statements concerning peace and the threat of nuclear weapons.[5] The ever-widening gap between the rich and the poor called for increasingly strong statements on the nature and the necessity for justice in the world.[6] The most recent example of this is the U.S. Catholic Bishops' pastoral letter, "Economic Justice for All," which explicitly applies Catholic social teaching to the U.S. economy.[7]

Although changing world conditions led to different emphases in the teaching, the basic convictions that faith must be active in the world and that Christian values must be brought to bear on contemporary questions remain constant. These teachings have provided an important source of inspiration and education—and sometimes controversy. One author's evaluation of the papal social teachings applies to the entire body of social teachings.

> (The social encyclicals) have formed over the past 90 years men and women who have found in them a charter to become concerned about institutional and structural reform, to support organization for justice, to heed the papal call to respect human dignity and to go to the poor. These men and women and the Catholic movements they have spawned are the best exegesis of the documents.
>
> Ultimately, the future of this tradition will depend less on our ability to parrot its significant terms such as subsidiarity, a just wage, socialization, or to define common good, and more on our ability to read the signs of the times in fidelity to the Gospel of human dignity as Leo, Pius XI, Pius XII, Paul VI—with all their historical limitations, biases and failures—tried to do in their times. History will surely unveil all too well our shortcomings. May it also — as it does for this legacy of the popes — show our prophetic vision and courageous action.[8]

The Church, as a global reality, lives in all types of neighborhoods throughout the world. It recognizes that its mission must be carried out in this world, and its leaders continue to call all people to care for the world and all who are part of it. One aspect of the Church's mission has received constant and growing emphasis: the need for justice and the recognition of our responsibility toward each other, especially those who are most in need.

JUSTICE

The United States is a country that takes pride in its system of justice. Our very foundation rests on the principles of "liberty and justice for all." We have a system of government that ensures representation for all citizens and a legal system that protects the rights of innocent people. We strive for fairness and struggle for equality, but we do not always reach our goals. A physician who works in a shelter for the homeless in Washington, DC, recounts an experience she had one night.

It was Christmas Eve. We had gone out in the van to attend to the people who try to stay warm by sleeping on the city's grates. I found myself on the street, kneeling next to a homeless man who had terrible burns on his legs and feet—from the steam coming up from the grates. I looked up and saw all the Christmas lights, the lights on the Capitol dome, the decorations at the White House. And I said to myself, "Something is terribly wrong here!"

This physician, and the homeless person she was trying to help, remind us of the generosity of our people and the flaws in our system. People reach out to help others, but there are so many in need, such disparity between groups. One of the reasons for this is an unbalanced emphasis on the individual.

We have seen that our faith tradition recognizes that all persons are made in God's image and are thus sacred. Each person is deserving of respect; each is of inestimable worth. When we think only in terms of individual worth, however, we fail to grasp the larger picture. Individual worth and dignity become "individualism," and the communitarian aspect of our reality is lost. A recent study of American cultural reality maintains that such individualism has become central to the American lifestyle.

Individualism lies at the very core of American culture. We believe in the dignity, indeed the sacredness, of the individual. Anything that would violate our right to think for ourselves, judge for ourselves, make our own decisions, live our lives as we see fit, is not only morally wrong, it is sacrilegious. Our highest and noblest aspirations, not only for ourselves, but for those we care about, for our society and for the world, are closely linked to our individualism.[9]

Individualism focuses on the self and often leads to blindness to others. It makes us incapable of recognizing the terrible contrast between a homeless man and elaborate decorations. It invites us to forget our responsibility to, and need for, each other. We fail to notice what happens in the neighborhood.

JUSTICE IN COMMUNITY

The biblical accounts that tell us we are made in God's image also tell us that we are made in relationship to each other. "It is not good that the man should be alone" (Gen 2:18). Creation is about relationship: a God who chooses to enter into relationship with humankind; a world in relation to itself and to God; human beings who stand unabashed before God and each other. Sin destroys relationships: the earth must be labored over; men and women hide from God and from each other.

The story of salvation is one of God's relentless pursuit of reconciliation with humankind and among humankind. St. Paul recognized this. When he wrote to the Christian community at Corinth, he chastised them because there were divisions among them. Such divisions, he said, denied the reality of what God had done in Jesus Christ since God had reconciled the world. "All this is from God, who through Christ reconciled us to himself and gave us the ministry of reconciliation; that is, in Christ God was reconciling the world to himself, not counting their trespasses against them, and entrusting to us the message of reconciliation" (2 Cor 5:18-19).

God gathered individuals and led them out of Egypt toward freedom. On the way to freedom, God formed a people. It is as a people that we are saved; it is as a people that we are called to know and serve the Creator. The essence of our identity as believers is our experience of belonging to each other. Each individual is of sacred value, but it is together that we reveal God's power to heal.

Justice and the Poor

The Gospel of John lovingly portrays the last evening that Jesus spent with his disciples. Chapters 13 to 17 show us a Jesus who washes the feet of his friends and who spends a long time talking with them, telling them where he is going, what will happen to them, and what he wants them to do and be. His command to them is that they love one another. This is how the world will know that they are *his* disciples: they love one another. "A new commandment I give to you, that you love one another; even as I have loved you, that you also love one another. By this all people will know that you are my disciples, if you have love for one another" (Jn 13:34-35). The love and care we have for each other are witness to the world of the loving God who acts to save.

That witness, enacted in people's lives and proclaimed in the Church's teachings, involves special attention to the poor and the vulnerable. It always has. Believers act in ways that mirror their understanding of the divine will for them. They act toward others in ways that mirror their understanding of the way God acts toward them. A fundamental insight of the Judaic-Christian tradition is that God comes to us in our weakness and vulnerability, in our poverty. "The Lord builds up Jerusalem; God gathers the outcasts of Israel. God heals the brokenhearted, and binds up their wounds" (Ps 147:2-3).

The entire Judaic-Christian tradition reveals a God who acts to save and heal those who are most in need. The book of Deuteronomy presents Moses' teachings to the people as they stood at the edge of the promised land. At one point, Moses reminds the people why God chose them among all the peoples of the earth. The text is really a summary of God's activity and the people's response. It reminds the people, and all who follow in their footsteps, that God does not choose on the basis of power and might.

> F or you are a people holy to the Lord your God; the Lord your God has chosen you to be a people for his own possession, out of all the peoples that are on the face of the earth. It was not because you were more in number than any other people that the Lord set his love upon you and chose you, for you were the fewest of all peoples; but it is because the Lord loves you, and is keeping the oath which he swore to your fathers, that the Lord has brought you out with a mighty hand, and redeemed you from the house of bondage, from the hand of Pharaoh king of Egypt. Know therefore that the Lord your God is God, the faithful God who keeps covenant and steadfast love with those who love him and keep the commandments to a thousand generations (Deut 7:6-9).

God chose the fewest of peoples, the poor, a nation's slaves. As we have seen, God made covenant with the people and gave them a law to live by. The law was not meant to restrict people's lives but rather to point to a way of living that manifested that *these* people were indeed God's people. "Central to this law was the care of the poor, usually the widows, orphans, and strangers among them [see Deut 24:19-22]. If the people were to be faithful to God, they had to show compassion to the most vulnerable in their midst. Such compassion was the way they showed their fidelity and manifested their identity as God's people."[10]

Heschel says that "God rages in the prophet's voice,"[11] and the prophets are well known for their rage. The focus of their rage, however, is the injustice of the people, especially the rulers. The poor were neglected and ignored. The widow and the orphan were not cared for by the leaders; the strangers were not welcomed into the land. Amos, a prophet in prosperous times, begins his teaching with the words, "The Lord roars from Zion!" (Amos 1:2). He berates the people because they "trample upon the poor" (5:11). Don't worry about the magnificence of your offerings, the majesty of your temple; these things won't help you before God, says Amos. Rather, "let justice roll down like waters, and righteousness like an ever-flowing stream" (5:24).

Amos represents a common and consistent voice in Israel's history, that of God's messenger who demands fidelity in justice. The prophet's words are echoed in the words of Jesus as he warns his disciples not to act as the Pharisees do. "They bind heavy burdens, hard to bear, and lay them on people's shoulders; but they themselves will not move them with their finger"

(Mt 23:4). The prophet's rage is matched in Jesus' rage: "But woe to you Pharisees! for you tithe mint and rue and every herb and neglect justice and the love of God" (Lk 11:42).

Jesus, born in poverty, reveals the intensity of God's love for the poor. Poor himself, he promised the kingdom to the poor. Having no place to lay his head, he nonetheless fed the hungry, called children into his presence and embraced them and returned sons to widows and children to grieving parents. One with the poor, Jesus made the place of the poor holy ground.

The place of the poor in our world, however, appears to be anything but holy. It is difficult to find God's presence in a grate that burns, in the crowded clinic, in the hospital that does not admit without insurance, or in the neighborhood that deteriorates before our unseeing eyes. The place of the poor is fraught with violence, hunger, and sickness. "Something is wrong," and what shall we do?

WHAT SHALL WE DO?

The Catholic healthcare ministry is rooted in a tradition that recognizes God's special love for the fragile in our midst and professes to continue that love. This tradition has expressed itself, particularly in the past century, in a series of statements, letters, and proclamations that emphasize our call to remain actively faithful to God's justice. "The obligation to provide justice for all means that the poor have the single most urgent economic claim on the conscience of the nation."[12] Response to this claim amidst the complexities of healthcare in the United States is often extremely difficult. If we are to be true to who we are, however, we must respond and lead others to respond. Many important steps are being taken; people are attending to neighborhoods and communities. Still, perhaps two primary acts must become habits for all of us.

In a scene in the gospel of Luke, Jesus' disciples return to him after missionary work. Sent out on their own for the first time, they were enormously successful, and even the demons were subject to them. They are filled with joy, and so is Jesus. Jesus rejoices because God has revealed such wonders to the little ones. Jesus praises God and then turns to the disciples and reminds them how blessed they are. He says, "Blessed are the eyes which see what you see! For I tell you that many prophets and kings desired to see what you see, and did not see it, and to hear what you hear, and did not hear it" (Lk 10:23). Perhaps we are called to hear and to see. Perhaps we will hear good news and see God's presence.

TO HEAR

In the late 1960s, inspired by the Church's social teachings, a group of women religious moved to an inner-city neighborhood to serve the poor. After they had been there nine months, the city erupted in riots. The women were in the middle of it. They stayed with the people until peace was restored. They continued to work with the people in the area for two more years. All who knew these women recognized their dedication and their commitment to justice. Some even envied them. They were clearly doing the Gospel. At the end of three years, however, these women left the inner city for new work. When asked why, they gave the following account.

W e went to the inner city to help the poor and the oppressed. We were committed to doing justice. Our education and our skills were excellent. We knew we could help. We did everything we knew to help the people. We held classes, we taught scripture, we went to city hall and to police stations, we visited homes. At one point—after about two years—we began to feel that we weren't really getting anywhere. We started to notice that people didn't really seem to trust us. One day we asked one of the few friends we had made why we weren't really making things better. "You want to make things better your way," he said, "and your way isn't our way." He continued: "You came down here to help us poor people. You had enthusiasm and dedication and lots of bright ideas. You knew what needed to be done and you went ahead and did it. Only problem was, you never asked us. You talked and talked to us and at us. But you never listened. You never heard what we said, you never asked our opinion. You made us feel poorer and stupider than we already felt. You want to help us? Then *listen* to us!"

We recognized the truth of his words. We decided to call a halt to our work—temporarily. We felt that we needed to learn how to listen, how to hear the words and the meanings behind the words before we could truly do justice. So, we're serving in other areas for awhile—and trying to learn how to hear.

We have seen that one of the most poignant phenomena of suffering is that it renders one mute. This is also true of poverty and oppression. The voices of the poor are muffled; they are not often heard in board rooms, in strategic planning sessions, or in values workshops. Mostly, the poor and the vulnerable go unheard until their voices are raised in rage.

To hear the cries of the poor, however, is at the heart of the Judaic-Christian tradition. The liberation of slaves in Egypt came about, we are told, because "the people of Israel groaned under their bondage, and cried out for help, and their cry under bondage came up to God. And God heard their groaning and God remembered the covenant" (Ex 2:23-24). God heard the cry and acted to save. Jesus heard cries and acted to heal. We saw in Chapter 2 how sensitive, efficacious listening is one of the characteristics of gospel healing. Recent social teachings have also stressed the importance of listening to the poor and the marginated.

In 1979, the Latin American bishops urged the Church to make a "preferential option for the poor."[13] The term, and the commitment it implies, has become basic in the Church's teachings since then. Two elements are included in this option: public witness of solidarity with the poor's struggle for justice and a commitment to view social reality from the perspective of the poor, the marginalized, and the powerless. "To view social reality from the perspective of the poor, it is necessary to enable the poor to speak. This aspect of preferential option calls the Church to listen, to be in solidarity with those who are often voiceless, and then to analyze society in terms of the forces that continue to victimize the poor. This implies that the poor have something to say, that they can teach us the gospel."[14]

Listening is an art; listening to the poor is both a gospel demand and a call to conversion.

TO SEE

One of the most consistent features of the Bible is the call to open our eyes and see. Those who do not believe are admonished with the words: "You see and see again, but do not perceive," while those who follow Jesus are told: "Happy are your eyes because they see" (Mt 13:14-16). The whole ministry of Jesus can be described as the gradual cure of human blindness, and all ministry in His name is the continuation of this healing task. Ministers are called to be seers who desire to help others see.[15]

The poor are not only mute, they are also invisible. Expressways divide cities and hide ghettos. Neighborhoods change, and we do not notice. Rural poor suffer hurricanes, and it takes months to find them. Young pregnant women with no insurance are first seen by a physician when they are about to give birth. Homeless people sit in parks, lie on grates, stand on corners, and yet remain invisible. Catholic healthcare givers need to see, however, and to see clearly. This can be a painful experience.

A recent film shows how seeing can transform our lives. *The Empire of the Sun* is the story of a young boy caught in the chaos of World War II. In an early scene, the boy is driven to his home in a chauffered car. As the car passes through the gates of his elaborate estate, the boy looks intently at a beggar who sits just outside the gates. The beggar pounds a box on the sidewalk and stares intently at the boy. This scene is repeated several times. Each time it is only the boy who notices the beggar. The others—chauffeur, maid, parents—do not see.

The rest of the film recounts the courage and ingenuity of a boy whose life is changed from that of a pampered, wealthy British colonialist to a survivor in a Japanese prisoner of war camp. Throughout the film, this boy sees too much. He sees what others miss, including the explosion of the first atomic bomb. At the end of the film, reunited with his parents, his eyes are glazed with sorrow.

It is often very painful to see clearly, because what we see makes demands on us. God heard the cries of the poor and saw their sorrow and acted to save. Prophets saw the injustices of their times and were forced to cry out. People in healthcare facilities recognize the changes in their neighborhoods and know they must act. A battered woman enters an emergency room, and people must see more than the broken limbs.

To truly see, one must see in layers. There is always more than surface reality. Family dynamics, societal conditions, living styles — all these are part of the reality. To truly see in the gospel sense, one must also have a vision. What appears before one now must appear in light of God's promise. There is nowhere that God will not go: into suffering, into death, into the lives and the faces of the poor.

Moses was an extraordinary man because he saw God face to face. Believers who truly see the poor, who look into their faces and their hearts, chance becoming extraordinary. However, it is not easy. "It is like the rabbinical story of a student asking 'In olden days there were men who saw the face of God. Why don't they anymore?' and the rabbi answering 'Because nowadays no one can stoop so low.'"[16]

There is something about the gospel, something about Christian life, that calls us to awareness and to involvement in our world. There is something in God's revelation that insists we hear and see and care for the poor. There is something that invites us to "stoop so low" and see the face of God.

Notes

1. Wayne A. Meeks, *The First Urban Christians: The Social World of the Apostle Paul,* Yale University Press, New Haven, CT, 1983, p. 1.

2. Raymond E. Brown, "Qumran," in Raymond Brown, et al., eds., *The New Jerome Biblical Commentary,* Prentice Hall, Inc., Englewood Cliffs, NJ, 1988, pp. 1069-1077.

3. Official papal letters, called "encyclicals," are usually named according to the first two words of the Latin text.

4. Peter Henriot, Edward DeBerri, Michael Schultheis, *Catholic Social Teaching: Our Best Kept Secret,* Maryknoll, NY, Orbis Books, 1988, pp. 20-22.

5. Pope John XXIII's encyclical "Peace on Earth" addresses this issue, as does the Vatican II document, "The Church in the Modern World," and the U.S. bishops' pastoral letter, "The Challenge of Peace: God's Promise and Our Response."

6. Three documents are particularly important in this area: the statements issued by the Latin American bishops at their 1968 meeting in Medellin, Columbia; their 1979 meeting in Puebla, Mexico; and "Justice in the World," the statement of the 1971 International Synod of Bishops.

7. "Economic Justice for All," Pastoral Letter on Catholic Social Teaching and the U.S. Economy, National Conference of Catholic Bishops, Washington, DC, 1986.

8. John Coleman, "Development in Church Social Teaching," in Charles E. Curran and Richard A. McCormick, eds., *Readings in Moral Theology,* no. 5, Paulist Press, New York, 1986, pp. 186-187.

9. Robert N. Bellah, et al., *Habits of the Heart: Individualism and Commitment in American Life,* University of California Press, Berkeley, CA, 1985, p. 142.

10. *The Poor Shall Teach Us: A Reflective Process on the Spirituality of Serving with the Poor,* Catholic Health Association, St. Louis, 1989, p. 14.

11. Abraham Joshua Heschel, *The Prophets,* Harper & Row Torchbooks, New York, 1969, vol. 2, p. 5.

12. "Economic Justice for All," no. 86.

13. For a further understanding of the evolution and the meaning of this expression, see Gregory Baum, "Option for the Powerless," *The Ecumenist,* November/December, 1987, pp. 5-11; and Thomas Clarke, "Option for the Poor: A Reflection," *America,* Jan. 30, 1988, pp. 95-99.

14. *Healthcare Leadership: Shaping a Tomorrow,* Catholic Health Association, St. Louis, 1988, p. 118.

15. Henri Nouwen, "The Monk and the Cripple: Toward a Spirituality of Ministry," *America,* March 15, 1980, pp. 205-210.

16. John S. Dunne, *The House of Wisdom: A Pilgrimage of the Heart,* Meyer Stone Books, Bloomington, IN, 1988, p. 20.

7

"The Earth Is Breathing Again"

STEWARDSHIP AND CATHOLIC HEALTHCARE

A young, native American woman ran into my office and cried: "Sister, Sister! You've got to come with me. Come now! You've got to see." She took my arm and started to pull me out the door. "See what?" I asked. She didn't answer, she just kept telling me I had to "come and see." So I did. We left my office, went down the corridor and out the back door of the building onto the parking lot. There was construction going on, and the workers had broken up the concrete covering the lot. "See," she said, "look!" I looked, but I couldn't see anything out of the ordinary. "The earth," she cried, "the earth is breathing again!"

This woman's experience reminds us of how far we can get from a sense that the earth is alive, that it needs to breathe. Her story calls all of us to look at the earth and recognize the amount of cement in our lives. Her account also reminds us that we need to care for our resources, to allow them to breathe.

Most of us do not attend to the earth's breathing every day. We are too busy driving on it, building on it, levelling it, or landscaping it. The complexity and the enormity of healthcare in the United States leave us little time to be in touch with the vast amounts of earth on which our facilities rest. Yet we continually make decisions about that earth, about its resources and ours. When boards of trustees approve operating budgets or capital expenditures, they are making decisions about resources. Administrators, trustees, sponsors, and financial officers all strive to be "good stewards." The decisions become increasingly difficult as the resources become increasingly scarce. How can we make wise decisions? Does faith play any part? Does the tradition offer us any help, any food for this part of the journey?

CREATION AND STEWARDSHIP

I t was the week after Christmas. A group of friends were having lunch. "So, what did you get for Christmas?" they asked each other. All the women gave the same general answers. They had each received the usual gifts. One woman, however, told of a special gift. "It's the most wonderful gift I've ever received," she said. "It's a quilt, but a very beautiful, very special quilt. I had seen it in a shop and had gone back to look at it for months. I could never afford to buy it. The quilt is made by the Hmoung women—Vietnamese refugees. I heard a story about them. When some of these women came to the United States, the Amish women helped them. They had quilting in common. Soon, the Hmoung women were teaching the American women how to do their kind of quilting.

"Anyway, I saw this quilt and loved it. My sisters came to town and I took them to see it. They, too, thought it was wonderful. They told me to buy it. But I couldn't. My sisters, though, did buy it—and surprised me with it at Christmas! Each time I look at it, I think about the woman who made it. I wonder where she is, what she thought as she stitched. I wonder if she would be happy that I have it. I wish she could know how much I cherish it and that I take good care of it. I also think about my sisters, their generosity and love for me.

"Like I said, it's the most wonderful gift I've ever received." She then announced that she was having a party—a celebration of the quilt.

All of us give and receive gifts. Every now and then, a gift is so perfect, so wonderful that we do not know what to say. It quickly becomes precious to us, an object (often something very simple) that reminds us of so much else. Creation is the original gift to all human beings. As with all gifts, it demands an appropriate response.

The biblical tradition begins with the story of creation. The first image of God is that of the Creator. "The only God that the Hebrew tradition knows is the God who is about the business of creating; that is, the Hebrew Scriptures contain nothing about God *in se,* God considered apart from the creating God."[1] The first image of man and woman is that of created persons whose very existence expresses an act of the Creator.

The Book of Genesis contains two accounts of creation (Gen 1:1-2:3; 2:4-24).[2] These accounts do not attempt to provide an historical description of the actual event of creation. They are, rather, theological statements that seek to articulate the meaning of human life and its relationship to God. They were written at different moments in Israel's history. Genesis 1:1 to 2:3 comes to us from the priestly tradition that was active in the sixth century BCE (Before the Common Era). It is a poetic description of a God who speaks ("And God said, let there be . .") and the universe being created. Creation takes place over six days, and the last to be created are human beings. They are, apparently, the culmination of God's work. Man and woman are made in God's image; that is, they are called to be the reflection of divine presence in the midst of creation.

Genesis 1:1 to 2:3 tells us that God blessed the woman and the man and gave them "dominion over the fish of the sea and over the birds of the air and over every living thing that moves upon the earth" (1:28). God entrusts the human beings with creation. They are to keep it and nurture it. Dominion does not mean an unthinking use of the earth's goods. It means, rather, a caring responsibility for them. Human beings are called by God to be co-creators: to continue the act of creation and to bring creation to its fulfillment.

This first account stresses the goodness of creation. The expression "and God saw that it was good," appears six times, a comment on each major act of creation. After everything had been created, we are told that "God saw everything that God had made, and behold, it was *very* good" (Gen 1:31). The writers of this account understood themselves and all creation as good. They show us a God who is pleased with all that exists. Further, they understood themselves as blessed, since God blessed the male and the female. Human beings, therefore, are blessed; they are in relationship with the Creator and are entrusted with the care of creation.

Genesis 2:4 to 24 provides another perspective on the meaning of creation. It is an earlier and more primitive account, coming to us from the Jahwist tradition (eighth century BCE). God is much more the active worker here. God forms the man from the dust of the earth and breathes life into him. Woman is created last, since God decides that it is not good for man to be alone.

This account portrays creation in terms of a beautiful garden that is given to the man and the woman to "till it and to keep it" (Gen 2:15). The human is told to name every living creature. To name something in biblical terms means to give it its identity. It also means to take responsibility for it. Human beings, we are told, are responsible for the garden and for everything that is in it.

Both accounts reveal an understanding of the meaning of human existence. Created by a loving God who was intensely involved in their creation, human beings know themselves as gifted with all creation, as responsible for it, as called to relationship with one another and with the God who saw that everything was good. Stewardship, responsibility to care for what is given to us, belongs to every human being as part of our reality as created persons. The breathing earth, the beautiful quilt, the joy we find in each other—all these are both gift and responsibility.

STEWARDSHIP TODAY

The gift and responsibility of creation work themselves out in history and within the context of human experience. Our responsibility for all creation becomes specified; the precious gift of creation is expressed in the specific gifts of our lifes. As participants in the Catholic healthcare ministry, the gift and responsibility of creation become specified in the gifts and responsibilities of healthcare's tradition and history and in the Catholic expression of that tradition. Both have been given to us; both have been entrusted that we might till them, nurture and cherish them, and cause them to grow.

> I remember the first day I walked in here as the new CEO. I was terrified. I stood outside the building for a few moments—it looked huge. The complexity and the enormity of the work I had agreed to do almost overwhelmed me. Then I saw that mural on the wall, the one about the founders. "How can I continue all of this?" I asked myself. "How can I ever carry on the traditions that these brave people started?" For awhile, I avoided that mural. It scared me. Then I began to get in touch with the spirit and the vision of the founders. I started to see how it was still alive, *and* how I could help to continue it. I'm still terrified sometimes, but the mural has become one of my favorite places. It helps me to remember, it gives me courage to risk.

We have inherited traditions and a ministry that can often be overwhelming. Both, however, are deeply connected with creation itself. Healthcare is a very special aspect of creation because it is about caring for human beings: nurturing the life that is in them, easing the pain that diminishes them, and accompanying them in their ultimate journey. Healthcare facilities rarely appear as the beautiful garden portrayed in Genesis. They are, however, places where we *reverence* God's image in our care for the dignity of the human person. They are also places where we *reveal* God's image in the way we creatively care for others. To care for others' lives is to enter into partnership with the God who gives all life.

The tradition of caring for the sick is as old as the biblical understanding of the God who heals and nurtures those in need. This understanding is confirmed in the gospels in Jesus Christ's actions. As God's image, Jesus reveals God's power and shows us that that power works to heal, to make whole, to straighten bent women, to return a widow's son to her, to heal a paralytic and return him to his friends.

The biblical tradition expresses itself within the Catholic tradition. As we saw in Chapter Two, the gift of healthcare is an expression of Catholicism's strong tradition of sacrament. St. Paul tells us that we are the body of Christ (1 Cor 12:12-31). We are, therefore, the manifestation of Christ in our world.

When we are true to who we are and are called to be, we are sacrament—revelation of God's healing presence. In our actions, it becomes possible to meet and be transformed by God's love. "A sacrament is not a stand-in for something else, a visible sign for some other invisible reality. The essence of a sacrament is the capacity to reveal grace, the agapic self-gift of God, by being what it is. By being thoroughly itself, a sacrament bodies forth the absolute self-donative love of God that undergirds both it and the entirety of creation."[3]

The Catholic tradition becomes further specified by the experience of Catholic healthcare in the United States. We have received as gift the spirit, courage, and daring of those who have gone before us. Catholic healthcare is a significant, constant factor in U.S. history. It began during the American Revolution and continues until today. Men and women, religious and lay, have always followed the call to heal the sick. They have always responded to the needs of their people, even when their people were perceived as the "enemy."

A t the start it was quite simply a response to social need.

Social need took many forms. Canadian sisters nursed American soldiers of Benedict Arnold's invading army. Sisters of two dozen communities served both Union and Confederacy, winning the praise of both Jefferson Davis and Abraham Lincoln. Sisters of one community, that of Our Lady of Mercy of Charleston, managed the huge Confederate hospital at White Sulphur Springs, while their care for federal prisoners in their home city was such that after the war General Benjamin "Beast" Butler became the staunch advocate of compensation to them for damages suffered in war. Sisters lost their lives in fever-ridden Florida camps, on hospital steamers returning the sick and wounded from Cuba and with the troops in Puerto Rico. In a final flourish, Daughters of Charity—blue habits, coronets, and all—staffed a hospital unit with the Allied Expeditionary Force on the Italian front in World War I.

The sisters' wartime experiences were dramatic, but their nursing forays were scarcely limited to the battlefields. They were there in epidemics that periodically swept American cities and they aided victims of fires, floods, and earthquakes. By rail and stagecoach, on horseback and on flatbed wagons, they traveled to minister to the builders of our railroads and in the gold-, silver-, and copper-mining boom towns of the West. Hospitals and clinics were opened and closed as miners moved on to the latest strikes. Sisters nursed those caught in explosions and cave-ins and, in the anthracite mines, those who were victims of black lung disease. Working among lumberjacks as the northern frontier moved west they introduced some of the earliest forms of medical insurance. They worked among Native Americans, blacks, and migrants. In modern times, Appalachia has been the scene of clinics and home-nursing services. In many parts of the United States communities unable to support hospital services were able to have them because a community of Catholic religious women were willing to take on the task.[4]

The stories, the spirit, the vision, and the ingenuity of women religious, men religious, and all the men and women throughout Catholic healthcare's history, are a vital part of our resources. They are gift to us — as inspiration, as challenge, as namers of the vision. They are also responsibility. How do we keep their vision alive in the world of the twenty-first century? How do we respond to the challenges of their ingenuity, creativity, and daring? How does their inspiration inform our decisions?

Stewardship, in terms of the U.S. Catholic healthcare ministry, involves tending to and nurturing our resources. These resources include the earth, the facilities that stand on the earth, the richness of a tradition that expresses itself in presence and sacrament, and the men and women who have gone before us. Our resources also include the women and men who are among us, who work with us, and for whom we care. How shall we be good stewards?

A WISE AND FAITHFUL STEWARD

We have seen that Jesus' parables are important and unique sources of wisdom and challenge. He told many stories about stewards and their roles, responsibilities, and failures. Stewards played a significant role in the culture of Jesus' time and were an important social grouping. A steward was responsible to the master; he[5] was entrusted with something by the master, usually while the master was away. The steward was responsible for whatever had been entrusted to him and was expected to give an account of his care for the master's resources. The roles of masters and servants were a major way in which the society organized itself. The relationship between master and servant or owner and steward was a voluntary one that implied long-term relationships in which respective roles and responsibilities were carefully defined. Even though these relationships were long-term, they were often unstable because they were based more on social custom than on law. The steward who thought he had been treated unjustly had no recourse in the legal system. The master was frequently isolated from the servants and was often an absentee landlord. This was especially the case in Galilee, the place of Jesus' ministry. The indigenous people were the poorest people and most often the servants. Jesus makes use of this reality when he tells his parables.

Two of Jesus' parables provide unique and surprising insights into the meaning of a good steward within the kingdom of God. When we try to hear the parables as the original hearers did, they challenge us to reexamine our own understandings and provide yet more food for our journey.

The first parable (LK 16:1-8a) is about a dishonest steward. In the story, the master is told that his steward is dishonest. He calls the steward and demands an accounting, then fires him. The steward leaves the master's presence and muses to himself. He tries to figure out what to do. He knows he cannot do physical labor, and he is unwilling to beg. He has a great idea. He goes to all the others who owe the master money and has them reduce the amount of their debts. He thus gains friends for the upcoming bad times even as he again cheats his master. The master receives word of this and calls the steward in again. The master then does a very disconcerting thing: he praises the dishonest steward.

This parable has embarrassed and confounded interpreters for centuries. It even embarrassed the early Christian community. The Lukan gospel adds several verses to the parable in an effort to soften the seeming contradiction it contains (vss. 8b-13).[6] How did the original listeners hear the parable? What can it say to us?

Those to whom the parable was spoken would have immediately identified with the steward. Jesus' hearers were poor people, those who knew what it was to be at the master's mercy. The steward is accused and not given a chance to defend himself. He is merely told that he is fired. A worker, hearing this, would probably say, "That's typical!"

In the second scene of the story, the steward does not deny that he has cheated his master. He also identifies himself with the rich. He cannot do manual labor and he is not willing to beg. The poor who hear this lose some sympathy for the steward because many of them would dig and beg. The steward then devises a plan. As he does so, he takes on the character of a scheming rogue. He could be compared to the villain in a Moliere play or in an old movie such as "The Perils of Pauline." As a clever rogue who gets even at the master's expense, the hearers once again begin to identify with him.

In the third act, the master confronts the steward. Those who are listening to the story expect that the master will be angry and punish the steward. Instead, he tells the steward that he has acted shrewdly and praises him. This throws everything off! In a culture where rules are rigidly observed, the master steps out of his role and becomes a dupe, a fool. What are we to make of this? In Jesus' culture, where power and justice were the same thing, the powerful person metes out justice ("you're fired"). Here, however, the unjust steward wins over the powerful master. How can this be?

The parable destroys the equation between power and justice. The powerful one is now the vulnerable one. The hearers, then and now, are bewildered. Is this how justice functions in God's kingdom? Is justice not used by the powerful to punish the unjust? And what of the steward? What are we to make of him? Has he really won? In commenting on this parable, one author states: "The kingdom is for the vulnerable, for masters and stewards who do not get even."[7]

Stewardship, according to this parable, is much more complicated than we would expect. It involves relationships between the one charged with caring for something and the one who truly owns that something. It calls for a certain understanding of power that is not domination over others, that is at ease with itself. Stewardship and ownership are not license to control or mandate to hold tightly. To be a good steward is not to act against or around the owner, whether the owner is in the office next door or is the ultimate owner.

The parable reminds us that the good steward is one who is open to the surprise of the kingdom, to the unexpected arrival and activity of God in our midst. We may—and must—take painstaking care of our resources. We may—and must—plan for their use and their preservation. We will, however, never have absolute security because God acts in most surprising ways. "Like a wise and prudent servant calculating what he must do in the critical reckoning to which his master summons him, one must be ready and willing to respond in life and action to the eschatological advent of God. But, unfortunately, the eschatological advent of God will always be precisely that for which wise and prudent readiness is impossible because it also shatters our wisdom and our prudence."[8]

> The board was furious. John Brown, the CEO, was at it again. They had hired him because he had a good track record; he'd helped save some hospitals that were in serious trouble. They hadn't known he was manipulative and sometimes less than honest. He was determined to make a name for himself, even at the expense of the hospital. Some board members found out (not from John Brown) that he had entered into negotiations to establish a transplant center at the hospital. There was already a famous transplant center in the area. This was not what the board had envisioned for the hospital.
>
> The board meeting was tense. John Brown was confronted about his actions and his dishonesty. They were ready to ask for his resignation. He did not appear to be very worried. Then something happened in the discussion. Anger and vengeance gave way. John Brown now uses his not inconsiderable gifts for the sake of the hospital. No one, least of all John Brown, expected this.

Good stewardship sometimes surprises us and challenges us to risk. Matthew and Luke both recount another parable about a steward and a master (Mt 25:14-28; Lk 19:12-27).[9] How shall we hear this parable? How did the original listeners hear it? In this parable, the master goes on a journey and entrusts his wealth to three different servants. The original listeners would immediately grasp the story line, much, as many would know the type of story that begins, "There was a travelling salesman…." The absentee landlord entrusts his property to his stewards, and the stewards will be put to the test. To the first he gives ten talents; to the second, five; and to the third, one. A talent was a great amount of money, more than 15 years' wages for a laborer. (It was also very large. One silver talent weighed between 57 and 64 pounds.)[10]

The first and second stewards go out and trade and make a profit. This would have been a normal action; the stewards stood to share in the profits they made. The third, however, takes the talent and buries it in the ground. The hearers would understand this. The steward had done the prudent thing; he will, they think, be shown to have been responsible. The master returns, and the moment of judgment occurs. Both the first and the second stewards have doubled their master's wealth. Both are praised and told: "Well done, good and faithful servant; you have been faithful over a little, I will set you over much; enter into the joy of your master" (Mt 25:21, 23). The meeting between the master and the third steward, however, is another matter.

This steward begins the conversation by characterizing the master as a "hard man, reaping where you did not sow, and gathering where you did not winnow" (Mt 25:24). He then says he was afraid of the master and that he hid the talent. Finally, he returns the talent to the master. The hearers would have sympathy for this man. Who would dare to risk the wealth of a hard man? The steward has done the prudent thing.

The master thinks differently. He calls the third steward wicked and slothful. He takes the talent from the steward and orders that it be given to the one who has ten talents. The hearers' opinions are confirmed: this man is unjust. However, there was nothing in the master's dealings with the first two stewards that indicated he was hard or unjust. These men gave no indication that they were afraid of their master. So, whom do we believe? How shall we be stewards in the kingdom?

An important Jewish tradition can perhaps provide a clue here. Israel believed herself blessed because she had received the Torah (the Law) from God. The Torah was precious and life giving for the people. It was the people's responsibility to guard and preserve it. This was especially true of the Pharisees. They were to "build a fence around the law." This could sometimes be a burden, as could the reception of a talent. There is a risk in overly careful preservation. One might close off the future.

The parable tells us that the one who buried the talent lost his future. It reminds us that stewardship is not always preservation, it is sometimes risk. "[I]n the parable it emerges how one goes about claiming the future. Is it claimed by preserving the precious gift? Or is it claimed in the present as freedom of action, liberating the servant from an aphoristic, conventional vision that paralyzes him? The parable as a window onto the kingdom demands that the servant act neither as preserver nor as one afraid; but act boldly he must."[11]

T he hospital was 80 years old. Its history was a distinguished one, its future fairly certain. The provincial council of the sponsoring congregation was in a quandary. A group of area residents had come to them with a plan that called for a radical refocusing of the hospital's mission. This plan, to set up a series of clinics in various areas, would change the nature of healthcare service the congregation had always provided. It would also be a very risky venture.

"We would be unfaithful to our charism," said one sister. "We could lose everything," said another. "We want to help the people, but running the hospital is what we have always done," said a third. Then something happened in the meeting. "Our charism is caring for the sick and the needy," they said. The fourth clinic opens next week.

The parables challenge our understanding of stewardship, even as they challenge our understanding of all we take for granted. When preservation and stability are the main manifestations of stewardship, have we perhaps lost sight of the gift and of the kingdom? Stewardship seems to demand a certain freedom to risk as well as a certain humility about power and control. It also demands intense attentiveness to the breathing of God's Spirit in our lives.

All human beings are called to stewardship. All are called to reverence and nurture the gifts given us by the Creator. All are called to hear the earth, to cherish it, and nurture it--and to remember that no one owns it. Participants in the ministry of U.S. Catholic healthcare are called to steward both the ministry's tradition and history and its present reality. This is an incredibly difficult task, a precious gift. How shall we be good and faithful? How shall we enter into joy? Perhaps the most important thing is to listen for the breathing of life in our midst.

Notes

1. Michael J. Himes and Kenneth R. Himes, "The Sacrament of Creation: Toward an Environmental Theology," *Commonweal,* Jan. 26, 1990, p. 45.
2. There are other accounts of creation in the scriptures, especially in the Wisdom literature (see, for example, Wisdom, Chapter 13). For an analysis of the creation accounts, see Richard Clifford, "Genesis," *The New Jerome Biblical Commentary,* Prentice Hall, Inc., Englewood Cliffs, NJ, 1988, pp. 8-13.
3. Himes and Himes, p. 45.
4. James Hennesey, "Prologue," Ursula Stepsis and Dolores Liptak, eds., *Pioneer Healers: The History of Women Religious in American Health Care,* Crossroad, New York, pp. 7-8.
5. In the patriarchal world of New Testament times, stewards were almost always men. Women were rarely entrusted with either responsibility or property.
6. For a detailed study of this and the following parable, see B. Scott, *Hear Then the Parable: A Commentary on the Parables of Jesus,* Augsburg Fortress Press, Minneapolis, 1989, pp. 255-266; 217-235.
7. Scott, p. 266.
8. John Dominic Crossan, *In Parables: The Challenge of the Historical Jesus,* Harper & Row Publishers, Inc., New York, pp. 119-120.
9. Although the gospel texts refer to "servants," the parable is about a steward, one who has been entrusted with the master's property.
10. Scott, p. 224. Luke's account refers to "minas" rather than talents. Although a mina represented less value than a talent, it was still a considerable sum.
11. Scott, p. 234. See also Dan Via, *The Parables: Their Literary and Existential Dimension,* Augsburg Fortress Press, Philadelphia, 1967, p. 119.

8

"It's More Complicated Than That"

MORAL LIFE AND HEALTHCARE

I had a 9 AM appointment, and I arrived early. There was a restaurant near the office, so I decided to go in and get a cup of coffee. I was startled to see a group of young women gathered around a table with several beer bottles. As I drank my coffee, I overheard their conversation. They were nurses who had just finished work and were relaxing a little before going home. They were talking about an elderly patient in a permanent vegetative state who had been taken off a respirator the night before. They had very mixed feelings about the event. One nurse said she didn't think that was ever the right thing to do. Another said that sometimes she thought it *was* the right thing to do. Still another said that it would always depend on the particular circumstances. As I finished my coffee and left the restaurant, I heard one say, "But it's more complicated than that!"

The ethical discussions present in the profession of healthcare today are undoubtedly complicated. The dilemmas often seem unresolvable. Such discussions must take place, however, and dilemmas must be resolved because people's lives are involved. Healthcare is always about people, many of whom frequently make difficult, complicated decisions. People are more than the decisions they make. They are a mysterious, marvelous combination of history, community, faith, choice, intellect, sexuality, imagination, sensitivity, hope, and anxiety. It is the whole person who makes decisions, who acts on those decisions, and who tries to do the right thing.

Moral theology is about persons in their totality, about the judgments they make and the actions they take. It implies a vision of what the world could be, of what is good and valuable. It rests on the belief that human persons are free and capable of making choices. It does not forget, however, that human freedom and human choices are strongly influenced by the worlds in which one lives. Each nurse in the opening story came to that table with his or her own history, faith tradition, experiences, and inherited sense of values. All of them encountered other histories, traditions, experiences, and values as they listened to their companions. Morality can never be separated from persons; it can only be demonstrated in the actions of human persons. But how does one become a moral person, how does one act morally? And what is the place of one's faith tradition in this process? Can the Catholic faith tradition guide and sustain us in the midst of confusing and often contradictory experience?

There is an assumption in the Catholic faith tradition that guides all discussion of morality. This assumption, present in the entire Judaic-Christian tradition, is that human persons are open to the experience of God. God calls us into life and continues to call us toward life. The continuous dynamic of God's call and our response are the basis for a moral life.

A s human persons, and all the more as Christians who understand the dignity and destiny of our world, we are called to goodness and responsibility. We experience ourselves as accountable, as challenged by ourselves and our world, as worthy of praise or blame depending on how we respond.

This call to be moral, moreover, makes itself heard across the length and breadth of our lives. No matter what the situation, no matter what the concrete issue, we experience ourselves as called and challenged by the real. We must do what is right. We must find and pursue the good. We must cultivate and nurture existence, we must be agents of creation and not of destruction. This is what it means to be moral.[1]

The Catholic tradition (together with other members of the Judaic-Christian tradition) seeks to articulate who we are as moral beings and how we should act within the context of this basic dynamic.

"WHO DO YOU SAY THAT I AM?"

Each of the synoptic gospels records a scene that most of us repeat several times in our lives. It involves a question of identity. Jesus has been with his disciples for awhile, has taught them, and has performed marvelous works in their presence. One day, he turns to them and asks what people are saying about him: who do they think he is? The disciples answer that some say he is John the Baptist, others say Elijah, others say one of the prophets. Jesus then asks the disciples, "But who do you say that I am?" (Mk 8:29; see also Mt 16:13-23; Lk 9:18-22). Peter answers, "You are the Christ."

Peter knows who Jesus is—the Anointed One, the Messiah. Jesus then tells the disciples what is to become of him. He predicts his own suffering and death. Peter, the one who knows Jesus' identity, rebukes Jesus for such talk (Messiahs do not suffer and die!). Jesus sharply rebukes Peter, making it clear that Peter does not really know Jesus as Jesus knows himself.

We all ask about who we are. We ask our friends what others think of us, what *they* think of us. Others' answers may deeply affect our perception of ourselves. A child who is constantly told he is stupid may come to believe that. Another who is told she is beautiful may presume that she is, despite what she sees in the mirror. If one is frequently called "bad," one may come to believe that, even though that person tries very hard to be "good."

The question of identity stays with us throughout our lives, since our identity develops throughout our lives. As we develop as persons, we should also develop as moral persons, capable of choosing and acting in ways that accord with our own vision of what is right or wrong.[2] Development always involves relationships. Every human being is born into some form of community. Family, school, neighborhood, city, and so on, all affect one's perception of the world. We quickly learn what a particular community values, what it considers good behavior.

M oral knowledge is embedded in group identifications we all have, associated with such distinctions as socioeconomic strata, race, age, and gender; it is embedded in nationality, cultural heritage, religious experience, family experience, and the institutions to which we belong. It resides in the larger patterns and systems of society that make up the material environment and cross over to the nonmaterial one: the economic order—local, regional, national, international; the governance system, and wielding of political power; the cultural system of social communication, with its major sectors in education, the mass media, and the numerous informal ways by which wisdom and instruction are passed from one circle and generation to the next, not least via family and friendship. In all of these, moral knowledge mirrors specific structures of dominance and subordination as well as mutuality, and of various and varying levels of privilege and deprivation as well as equality and reciprocity.[3]

This visible world and the less tangible world of powerful ideas, social vision, and commonly held world views shape us and form our character. Human beings are not totally passive in their worlds. Children quickly learn to say, "No." Adolescents frequently rebel against a family's world to be part of their peers' world. Visionaries and prophets judge and seek to transform their worlds. It is in the interaction between the person and his or her social world that development takes place and character is formed: "... *moral character is formed in this interactive process*. It occurs in a communal process of specific, changing, and continuing social relations. *'Character' is the name given to the moral being of a person or group as that is forged into a distinctive constellation.*"[4]

When a nurse says that she could never perform a particular action and an administrator says that she could never act as her predecessor, they are expressing the reality of their characters. To act in a particular way would be to go against who they are. Rejection of redemptive suffering by Jesus would have denied who he was, no matter what Peter thought.

We may never explicitly discuss a person's character, but we recognize it when that person does not adhere to it. The patient who is harshly treated by a usually sensitive physician may ask that physician what is wrong: "You're not yourself today." An alert caregiver may detect a change in a person's physical condition because that patient is not "acting like himself."

"Who do you say that I am?" Our worlds will give us many answers. We will give our own answer. It is important to remember that the worlds' answers and our answers are never given in isolation from each other. Also, they are never complete answers, since we never stop growing and developing and neither do our worlds.

Because our worlds constantly change, one never absorbs *all* one encounters. Selective hearing and selective vision are part of every life.[5] Two people may hear the same piece of news at the same time and arrive at two entirely different conclusions. Each of us has a perspective on life, and that perspective influences how we absorb and integrate what enters our life. Further, our character is expressed in our dispositions and intentions. *Dispositions* are habitual responses. If I am usually kind, kindness becomes a habit, and I act "out of character" when I am cruel. *Intentions* refer to the aim or purpose of my actions. I can be kind because I have compassion on another *or* because I want to fool another. Kindness in a devious person operates for a different reason than kindness in a loving person.

Our moral character, expressed in dispositions and intentions, is closely linked with conscience. Many of us first learned about conscience from Saturday morning cartoons. "Conscience" is usually the little character sitting on the child's shoulder telling him to be good or urging her not to throw the rock or play in the street. In these scenarios, conscience most often loses to the more exciting "temptation" that sits on the other shoulder. Conscience is neither outside the person nor a "little voice" inside a person's head. "But most basically conscience is a special kind of personal consciousness. It is the awareness of oneself as a morally responsible being who can be called to account not only by one's fellow human beings, but by one's own inner self, and, in religious terms, by God. In this sense conscience is basically *the person as morally conscious.*"[6]

Just as the person grows and develops, one's conscience must grow and be allowed to develop. Frequently, such development takes the form of a call to conversion.[7] New information and new sensitivities lead us to new perceptions. We may change our minds or, more importantly, our hearts. Birch and Rasmussen recount an experience of conversion. A severely disabled young man addressed a group of physicians who were attending a conference on the ethics of organ transplants. He spoke to them about ancient societies' practices of killing disabled persons. This same practice continues today, he said. When challenged by the audience, he asked a question. "If two persons could avoid death, and could anticipate significantly prolonged life from an organ transplant, and if the only difference between them was that one was disabled and the other not, who would receive the saving transplant?" The physicians defended their practice with reason and intelligence. Slowly, however, the group began to realize that, according to their reasoning, the young man in front of them would not have been given a transplant. "The surgeons experienced a kind of slow, silent moral shock. Deep down they realized they had not considered the disabled to be fully persons."[8] This "moral shock" inevitably leads to conversion—a recognition of the inadequacy of their former understanding, a turning to a deeper understanding.

Most conversions are less dramatic than this. They may consist of the recognition that certain employment policies are unjust and a decision to change those policies. They may appear in the acknowledgment that healthcare facilities are responsible for the environment in which they exist, with the ensuing decision to stop using nonbiodegradable elements such as Styrofoam in a healthcare system. Nurses gathered around a restaurant table may hear new information and face new challenges that will lead to re-formed perspectives. As moral persons, we are constantly invited to deepen our understanding and be more faithful to our vision.

Continuing conversion develops virtue. Virtue, at its most basic, is a human capacity. Moral virtue "is the power (ability, skill, facility) to realize moral good, and especially to do it joyfully and perserveringly even against inner and outer obstacles and at the cost of sacrifices."[9] This power does not come about without work. Virtue, too, is developed. Our actions enhance our ability to do something; our skills must be used or they will deteriorate. Acting with moral integrity becomes a habit; we do not stop and think each time we speak truthfully or act justly. An honest person is habitually honest, and dishonesty is "out of character" for that person.

Moral virtues also refer to those qualities and character traits that are valued and prized within a given community. They refer not only to individual character, but also to the social reality. What are the qualities that will enhance our living together? What will make for a just and generous society? Will we be truthful with each other in this organization? Will we respect each other and our patients? Will you treat me with reverence even when I am in pain and diminished by illness?

"Who do you say that I am?" How we answer this question involves many factors: our character and how it has developed within our personal and social histories, our conscience as it is more or less open to conversion, the capacity we have to choose and to act for the good and our openness to God's call in our lives. Our whole being is involved in living rightly, and our being is best revealed in our actions.

"GO AND TELL"

Matthew and Luke both recount another event where Jesus' identity was questioned (Mt 11:2-19; Lk 7:18-35). In this case, the imprisoned John the Baptist sends his disciples to Jesus to ask: "Are you he who is to come, or shall we look for another?" (Lk 7:19). Jesus answers, "Go and tell John what you have seen and heard: the blind receive their sight, the lame walk, lepers are cleansed, and the deaf hear, the dead are raised up, the poor have good news preached to them" (7:22). Jesus tells who he is by pointing to what he does.

So do we. We are often (and unfortunately) categorized by what we do, what is our work or profession. What we do frequently determines our social status, neighborhood, and income. There is, however, a deeper way in which our actions reveal our identity, a way in which "our actions betray us." Our actions reveal our character. A chief executive officer's words about the importance of collaboration may be "betrayed" by her engagement in ruthless competition. A physician's verbal commitment to compassion can be denied in his refusal to accept uninsured patients. Morality resides in who we are, but it lives in what we do.

Individuals and societies act in function of their values: the moral goods that persons wish to see actualized in their worlds. Gloria Naylor provides a fascinating study of how values influence the life of communities in her two novels, *The Women of Brewster Place*[10] and *Linden Hills*. Brewster Place and Linden Hills are two neighborhoods separated by a brick wall. Brewster Place is poor; Linden Hills is wealthy. For the women of Brewster Place, caring for each other is vitally important. They support each other in pain and work together to energize the community. Their grief at the vicious attack on one of the women finds communal expression in tearing down the wall that encloses them. Their values are those of caring: caring for others, caring about their community.[11]

Linden Hills is famous throughout the country for its wealth. Its residents prize money, prestige, and respectability. People in Linden Hills compromise their integrity and deny their consciences to sustain their existence there. Each in turn is destroyed. The story of Linden Hills is a dramatic tale of the tragedy of wrong values and the terror in the power of compromise with evil.

How character expresses itself in the pursuit of values can also be seen in real life. The response of the community, especially the healthcare community, of Sioux City, IA, to the crash of United Airlines' Flight 232, July 19, 1989, is eloquent testimony. Sioux City prides itself on being a community where people care about one another. Their caring became an outpouring of compassion at the time of the plane crash. The newspaper accounts of the crash focused as much on the generosity of the people of Sioux City as on the crash itself. Some examples:

> Investigators continue to look into the crash of United Flight 232 last week in Sioux City, Iowa. But we've already learned about the heroism displayed by many of the people involved. In these times of contagious cynicism, such actions remind us that humans have a greater calling. (Irving, CA, newspaper)
>
> "We never put out an emergency call," said Kenneth Lawson, executive director of the Sioux City blood center. "People just started appearing at our door." *(Kansas City Star)*
>
> Johnson (Doug Johnson, president of Marian Health Center) marveled at the unity of the city, which is a processing center for beef, pork and grain. "It's united most of the time, but boy, during a crisis, it's really united," Johnson said. *(Arizona Republic)*

The reflection printed in a special edition of *Marian,* a magazine published by Marian Health Center in Sioux City, speaks movingly to values in action: preparedness, caring for others who need us, lovingly touching others —healthcare as we hope it will be. "Our actions on that day and those that followed are, for us, a condition of being alive and connected to others. And so when others want to call us heroes, we are polite but our instinct is to argue and say no. We were prepared, it's true. We did our jobs, that's true too. And we lovingly touched others. But how could we not? And how can that make us heroes?"[12]

The people of Sioux City responded to the obligations laid on them by the "condition of being alive and connected to others." Because we always live in relationship with others, it is necessary to respect certain duties and obligations to maintain our life together.

People in a healthcare facility, for example, need to maintain a basic truthfulness. If we cannot believe a physician's diagnosis, how can we give proper care? All persons must offer one another a basic human respect; otherwise, people become objects open to manipulation and mistreatment. The Golden Rule, treat others as you would have them treat you, is not merely a suggestion for the good life. It allows society to continue with a modicum of ease and equity. Moral obligations are claims upon us by the very fact that we are human beings in relationship with others.[13]

Many people, however, do not act according to moral obligations. Some persons respect no one, and their word cannot be trusted. Whole societies have denied basic human respect to various classes of human beings; governments have functioned through secrecy and intimidation. The rejection of obligation and the prizing of vice instead of virtue are possible because human beings are free. We are able to choose what we will cherish, to respond or not to the claims of others. Our freedom to choose is fiercely defended in American culture. It is the very foundation of U.S. ethos. At the same time, not everyone has had the same freedom, not all have been given choices in matters basic to their lives. The denial of freedom and the refusal of respect often result from a distorted moral vision. Our vision of the good society influences who we are and what we do. It is vitally important to name that vision, test it against other visions, and remain faithful to it as we work to achieve it.

A QUESTION OF VISION

The gospels provide us with a dramatic example of conflicting visions. After his baptism, Jesus was led by the Spirit into the wilderness. He fasted for 40 days and nights, "and afterward he was hungry" (Mt 4:1; Lk 4:2). The devil comes to Jesus to tempt him. The temptations are threefold, and each represents a vision of life. The first is the use of power to satisfy one's own needs: turn these stones into bread. The second is the misuse of God's protection: "If you are the Son of God, throw yourself off this pinnacle" (Mt 4:6; Lk 4:9). The third is to worship evil so that one may possess all the riches of the world.

In each case, Jesus rejects the temptation and the tempter. He refuses to use power selfishly; he refuses to "tempt God." He will worship God alone. Jesus, filled with the power of the Spirit, remains faithful to a vision, one he expresses in the Beatitudes, one that eventually leads to his death. "What the Son would not take from Satan's hands at the cheap price of idolatry he has won for himself at the cost of the cross."[14]

Moral vision is fundamental to moral life. It is both beginning and end point. "Moral vision is the vision of the good we hold, a part of which is how we perceive ourselves and regard ourselves and others. It is our integrated grasp of the moral realm."[15] Our vision of the meaning of life and of the human reality shapes our judgments of what is good and evil and influences our actions toward the realization of the good. We begin with a vision, one inherited from previous generations. As we grow, we respond to that vision with enthusiasm or with challenges. The vision is always the end point: how does this act or this choice accord with or contradict the vision? Without a vision of the whole, the moral life risks becoming a series of disconnected acts, a set of unrelated principles, a list of virtues. Moral vision provides the context in which I work out who I am and how I am to act.[16] It also provides the context in which the community discovers its meaning.

It is especially in terms of moral vision that the Judaic-Christian tradition provides insight and challenge and gives us food for the journey. The vision of the meaning and responsibilities of human existence revealed in the Judaic-Christian tradition shapes our lives and judges our actions. We have seen by now how very rich that tradition is, how wide and gracious its vision. Certain aspects of that vision are vitally important in helping us to understand ourselves as moral beings and to act in ways that are faithful to that understanding. These are community, covenant, the future, and worship.

COMMUNITY

The director of nursing was having a discussion with a physician. It seems that the physician had been less than cooperative and unreasonably demanding in his relationships with the nursing staff. The physician made it clear that he did not like "the way you do things around here." The director of nursing insisted that courtesy and cooperation were expected of everyone, including the medical staff. She commented on the physician's behavior and said, "We simply do not act that way here."

One of the ways we recognize that someone has begun to feel at home with a group or an organization is the use of language. One moves from talking about "you" to speaking of "we." The physician in the above incident thought of himself as separate from the hospital community, whereas the director of nursing expressed her membership within that community. The language of both Judaism and Christianity is the language of "we." The moral discourse is a discourse of "we."

The experience of salvation expressed in both the Hebrew scriptures and the Christian gospels is a people's experience. The articulation of a code of behavior and way of life is the articulation of what "we" shall do, how "we" shall live. "The beginning experiences for both Jewish and Christian ethics are the experience of God as the One who generates community and the One who is experienced *in* community, as its deepest source and meaning."[17] The communities' experience of God, whether in the desert of the Exodus or the houses of the early Christians, led them to formulate a way of life that they believed was in keeping with the God they knew. Because God had mercifully freed them in their poverty, they in turn must be sensitive to the poor among themselves. Because God had brought them together as a people, they must remain a people. Because God had shown them compassion, they must have compassion for one another. Because Jesus had loved them so deeply and so completely, they must love one another.

Ideally, Christian morality is the expression of Christian vision. It concretizes our experience of the loving, merciful God. It is the expression of the community's understanding and commitment. Morality's basic question is not "What must I do?" but rather, "Given what we have experienced, how shall we live?" We saw in Chapter 4 that community is vital in our understanding of and response to suffering. More than that, however, community is central to our identity and our moral vision. It is only when we understand ourselves as a people who belong to one another that we can begin to understand how we must live and what choices we must make, since all our choices affect all of us.

Decisions and actions in healthcare, whether they concern the proper care of a suffering person, the quality of relations among staff, the purchase of equipment, or a facility's expansion or closing, must always be viewed in terms of the community and its needs. How will what we do affect us as a people? How clearly do our actions affirm our identity?

COVENANT

We have seen that one way to express our identity is to speak of ourselves as a people of covenant.[18] We are people who have accepted the invitation of God and have entered into faithful relationship with that God. Covenant continues that relationship and constantly reminds us that *God* is involved. It also reminds us that our whole lives are involved.

May finds the image of covenant to be central to a physician's life and work and to a healthcare institution. He speaks of three elements in covenant: an original gift, a promise based on the gift, and the acceptance of an inclusive set of ritual and moral obligations by which covenanted people live.[19] Covenant involves personal identity but does not allow us to separate ourselves into various "roles."

C ovenants cut deeper into personal identity. A contract has a limited duration, but the religious covenant imposes change on all moments. A mechanic can act under a contract, and then, when not fixing a piston, act without regard to the contract; but a covenantal people acts under covenant while eating, sleeping, working, praying, cheating, healing, or blundering. Paul remarks, in effect: When you eat, eat to the glory of God, and when you fast, fast to the glory of God, and when you marry, marry to the glory of God, and when you abstain, abstain to the glory of God (1 Corinthians 10). Initiation into a profession means, in effect, that the physician is a healer when healing and when sleeping, when practicing and when malpracticing.[20]

Just as the image of community reminds us that we cannot make decisions in isolation from others, the image of covenant tells us that healthcare givers cannot comparmentalize themselves. The administrator cannot be generous and compassionate at home or in church and yet be hostile and demanding at work. Healthcare leaders cannot make some decisions because they are "good for business" and others because they are "faithful to the mission." Covenant implies integrity and consistency—in all aspects of the moral life.

THE FUTURE

Both community and covenant are dynamic realities. They imply history, development, and a future. So does the moral life. The person grows and develops within moral life's various communities, makes choices with greater knowledge and wider experience, and makes judgments that are more informed. As long as one is alive, growth is possible; the future promises new possibilities. Within the biblical tradition, another sense of future is that of God's future.

The story of God and the people is one that always begins with God's initiative. God calls a people; God calls each person. That call is always toward greater fulfillment, greater integrity. God's people have always recognized that fulfillment and integrity are only partially realized. Paul's realization that "sin dwells in me" is everyone's realization. We all say, "For I do not do the good I want, but the evil I do not want is what I do" (Rom 7:19). A sober recognition of the evil that lives in us and in our world is of the essence of the moral life, but it is not the sum of the moral life.

Combined with the recognition that true fulfillment is only partially realized is the belief that one day it will be fully real. The biblical story is about people on a journey, people who have been promised God's goodness, who have glimpsed it partially, and who are enabled to continue on toward the final point. Profound belief in the future God has promised gives rise to the basic optimism of the biblical tradition. This belief allows Paul to say, in the midst of life's anguish, that "in all these things we are more than conquerors through him who loved us" (Rom 8:37).

Belief in a future leads to the building of that future. Visions of helping people, curing disease, and eliminating unnecessary deaths are the stories of healthcare. The visions urged people to their realization. Hospitals, clinics, vaccines, and new therapies exist because someone believed they *could* exist. In the same way, the believing community looks to a future when God will be all in all and struggles to help that future to become a reality. The community's development as a community of moral integrity is always guided by its vision of the future. The Christian moral vision must always take the future into account; it must derive its inspiration, its hope, and its energy from the promised future. The journey continues, and nourishment is available along the way.

WORSHIP

When God called Moses to begin the journey of the Exodus, God told him the sign showing that Moses had indeed been sent by God: "When you have brought forth the people out of Egypt, you shall serve (worship) God upon this mountain" (Ex 3:12). Worship of the God who saves is essential to the journey. Miriam took up timbrel and praised the God who led the people through the waters (Ex 15:20-21). The bent woman, healed by Jesus, stood up straight "and praised God" (Lk 13:13). Fidelity to the journey demands recognition and praise of the One who accompanies. Worship is such recognition and praise. In worship, the people remember the God who saves; they give thanks and acknowledge their dependence on this God. Worship reminds us of who we are and who God is.

Worship also shapes and forms a people. It is through meaningful liturgical experience that the faith story is told and translated in terms of contemporary reality. Liturgy both teaches and reminds us of the call to discipleship. Ultimately, it leads us to encounter with the One we claim to follow. Celebration of Eucharistic liturgy remembers and relives the Paschal mystery. It unites us with the Savior and with one another. Eucharist feeds us, gives us sustenance for our lives. "The further reach of moral activity is prayer. The turning to the Ultimate Other demands and empowers the recognition and response to its incarnate presence in the neighborhood."[21]

"It's more complicated than that." The moral life is indeed a complicated one. It involves our character, our vision, our history, the various communities in which we live, and the life of worship in our faith community. Ultimately, the moral life is a life in faith. It is response to the invitation of God. It is fidelity to the journey.

Notes

1. Timothy E. O'Connell, *Principles for a Catholic Morality,* Seabury Press, Minneapolis, 1978, p. 163.
2. Much research and discussion has taken place in the area of moral development. For a discussion of various theories and their relationship to moral theology, consult James W. Fowler and Antoine Vergote (senior authors), *Toward Moral and Religious Maturity: The First International Conference on Moral and Religious Development,* Silver Burdett Company, Morristown, NJ, 1980. See also Philip S. Keane, *Christian Ethics & Imagination,* Paulist Press, Ramsey, NJ, 1984, pp. 153-161.
3. Bruce C. Birch and Larry L. Rasmussen, *Bible & Ethics in the Christian Life,* Augsburg Publishing House, Minneapolis, 1989, p. 72.
4. Birch and Rasmussen, p. 74 (italics in the original text).
5. One has only to recall the reaction of Lila when the physician told her of her cancer. See Chapter 2, pp. 31 & 32.
6. Sean Fagan, "Conscience," Michael Glazier, Inc., Wilmington, DE, 1987, *The New Dictionary of Theology,* Joseph Komonchak, Mary Collins, and Dermont Lane, eds., p. 227. (italics in the original text)
7. Conversion is a central theme in contemporary moral theology. See Charles E. Curran, *Moral Theology: A Continuing Journey,* University of Notre Dame Press, Notre Dame, IN, 1982, especially pp. 72-74 and the references cited.
8. Birch and Rasmussen, p. 58. The authors describe this experience in terms of an expansion of moral vision. Such expansion undoubtedly led to the beholders' conversion.
9. Bernard Haring, "Virtue," Karl Rahner, Ed., *Encyclopedia of Theology: The Concise Sacramentum Mundi,* Crossroad, New York, 1975, p. 1794.
10. Gloria Naylor, *The Women of Brewster Place,* Penguin Group, New York, 1982, *Linden Hills,* Penguin Books, New York, 1985.
11. The *Women of Brewster Place* portrays in fiction what Carol Gilligan has proposed in academic research: women develop through relationships and live with an ethic of caring. See Carol Gilligan, *In a Different Voice: Psychological Theory and Women's Development,* Harvard University Press, Cambridge, MA, 1982.
12. This statement and preceding newspaper citations from *Marian* magazine, special edition, Marian Health Center, Sioux City, IA.
13. Birch and Rasmussen, pp. 52-58.

14. John P. Meier, *Matthew,* New Testament Message, vol. 3, Michael Glazier, Inc., Wilmington, DE, 1980, p. 31.
15. Birch and Rasmussen, p. 59.
16. Keane stresses the importance of imagination in the formation and development of the moral vision, pp. 64-70. See also Stanley Hauerwas, *Vision and Virtue: Essays in Christian Ethical Reflection,* Fides Press, Notre Dame, IN, 1974.
17. Birch and Rasmussen, p. 19.
18. Chapter 4, pp. 64-66.
19. William F. May, *The Physician's Covenant: Images of the Healer in Medical Ethics,* The Westminister Press, Philadelphia, 1983, pp. 108-109.
20. May, p. 119.
21. Enda McDonagh, "Moral Theology and Moral Development," *Toward Moral and Religious Maturity,* James Fowler, Antoine Vergote, senior authors, Silver Burdett Company, Morristown, NJ, 1980, p. 341.

EPILOGUE

LIVE BY THE WORD AND KEEP WALKING

Alice Walker begins one of her recent books with a description of a dream she had. In the dream, a two-headed woman appeared to her. "A wise woman. Stout, graying, caramel-colored, with blue-gray eyes, wearing a blue flowered dress. Who was giving advice to people. Some white people, too, I think. Her knowledge was for everyone and it was striking."[1] Alice Walker asked this woman if the world would survive. The woman said no. When Alice asked her, "what I/we could/should do," however, the woman picked up her walking stick and walked "expressively and purposely across the room." She said: "Live by the Word and keep walking."

It is hoped the discussions in this book have enabled us to see more clearly that life is a journey and that food is needed for that journey. Even God's prophets cannot walk forever without food. Reflection on the riches of our tradition and on the inexhaustible Word of God nourishes and sustains us, even as it calls us to keep on walking. We have seen that we do not walk unaccompanied, but that the divine goes with us, and that we always journey together. God is present in human experience, transforming both it and us. In our journey, we have come to recognize that healthcare is a ministry deeply rooted in the mission of Jesus Christ himself. When we reach out to touch in compassion, we act as disciples and reveal the saving compassion of our God. Catholic healthcare is a ministry within the Catholic Church. The Church is the vehicle that allows for the continuation of healthcare as ministry, especially through the lives and inspiration of the men and women who have preceded us and who accompany us. The Church is the "house" in which we dwell; it nourishes us, and from it we are sent forth to serve.

Catholic healthcare, enlivened by God's presence, exists in the midst of suffering and death. The journey is difficult here, the land dry and barren. The tradition, however, offers nourishment: suffering is not endured alone; death is not the final victor. The tradition we have inherited is part of the richness of the resources for which we must care. Understanding stewardship leads us to recognize that all our resources—material, historical, human, religious--must be cherished, nurtured, and ultimately placed before the One true owner.

Catholic healthcare, continuation of God's healing presence, takes place in the world. It is not an isolated entity, pursuing its goals aloof from the neighborhoods in which it exists. Because of this, we are responsible for those neighborhoods. The Church's social teachings both guide and challenge us here; they give wisdom and "food for thought." These teachings, and the biblical traditions from which they rise, remind us that it is especially the poor who call us, who are both grace and call for us.

Throughout the journey, we recognize that healthcare is always about persons and persons in community. It is in the dynamic between persons that healthcare takes place. As persons, open to one another and to God, we are called to be and to act morally. The choices we make, the actions we do, the types of people we are—all these spring from our vision of life. The tradition helps shape that vision, helps us to see more clearly and faithfully.

Great riches exist in the Judaic-Christian tradition. There are many foods for our journey. Some are to be savored, tasted slowly and lovingly. Others are more difficult to digest, they might need to be swallowed with courage. All nourish us; however, all give us strength to journey together for the sake of those we serve, to "live by the Word and keep walking."

Neither books nor knowledge alone will keep us walking. There is yet one more necessity: the ongoing relationship between ourselves and the One who goes with us. We are people with moral capacities; we are also people with spiritual capacities. Ultimately, it is the spirituality of the healthcare professionals and of the healthcare communities that will make our journey one of grace and graciousness.

McCormick calls for a spirituality for healthcare personnel. "By *spirituality* I refer to a personal and corporate life-climate designed to foster and deepen belief in and insight into the basic structure of our lives as revealed in God's self-disclosure in Jesus, and particularly as this is encountered in the medical context."[2] Spirituality is a word with many overtones. For some people, it means the mysticism of the monks; for others, it means the latest fad; for others, it means nothing at all. "However, every believing person has a spirituality. More correctly, every believing person lives within the context of a spirituality. At its most basic, spirituality is the way in which an individual or a community experiences and responds to the activity of God in everyday life."[3]

If even a brief study of the Judaic-Christian tradition tells us anything, it tells us that human beings can be in relationship with God. We can, as the Baltimore Catechism taught us, "know, love, and serve God." This knowledge transforms us, sustains us, delights us, and challenges us. Spirituality is the name we give to the ongoing process of knowing and responding to God in our lives. Because we come to know God in human experience, our experience both gives a certain flavor to that knowledge and asks certain types of response. For example, if my experience of parental authority is one of harshness and punishment, my understanding of God the Father may be one of a harsh and demanding judge. I will probably be very careful before this God and eager to avoid his punishments. If, on the other hand, my parents are loving, forgiving people whom I trust, God for me may be loving

Father/Mother to whom I turn for help and forgiveness. I will not be afraid of this God.

Spirituality is intensely personal; it is also communal. The Exodus people came to know God in their common experience of liberation. The early Christians proclaimed the resurrection after their mutual experience of Pentecost. Healthcare personnel have spiritualities, but so do healthcare institutions. We must always ask: "How is God present in the working of this place? Where is God working in our decision making, in our strategic planning? How is God revealed in our care?" McCann makes a strong case for the importance of spirituality for healthcare institutions marked by American individualism and often in the midst of crisis.

> Unless spirituality is recognized first as an essential condition of the institution's own ongoing life, the institution will hardly be powerful enough to understand, let alone resist, the opposite set of half-truths contained in utilitarian individualism. In short, unless spirituality is properly understood as a function of the institution as such, it can hardly be regarded as relevant to the crisis precipitated by the monetarization of health care policy.[4]

Spirituality, personal and communal response, will have specific characteristics that reflect the lived experience of both individuals and communities. What would be some of the characteristics of a spirituality for persons and communities involved in healthcare? Many exist, but our journey to this point suggests three: wonder, humility, and perseverance.

WONDER

We have seen that the crowds were astonished by Jesus. They were amazed by his power to heal. They pondered and were puzzled; they questioned and rejoiced. In the healed woman, the seeing man, the cleansed leper, and the raised Lazarus, they saw God's power at work. How could they not be astonished?

We have seen, too, that human beings are made in the image of God and are sacred. One must stand in awe before this creature that bears God's life in our world.

Healthcare strives to heal, and in so doing reveals again God's power. Healthcare touches human beings; it carries God's image in its hands. It is sacred work that takes place on holy ground. How can we not be astonished, how can we not wonder at the holy in our midst?

Wonder is more than curiosity. It is, in the words of Heschel, "radical amazement."[5] To wonder is to recognize the presence of mystery in life, to view life within the horizon of the divine. Wonder is the sigh, the "oh!" of astonishment. It is amazement that we are who we are, "wondrously made" (Ps 139), and that creation is filled with the presence of the divine.

The dramas *and* the routines of healthcare are at the very heart of the mystery of creation. Assisting in birth, accompanying in death, healing broken limbs, easing pain—these are of the essence of life. To be part of such work is to be invited to wonder. It is a call to stand back and to recognize the sacred and the sacredness of our calling. In today's slang, we can say that healthcare is "awesome," and awe is vitally important to us. "Awe enables us to perceive in the world intimations of the divine, to sense in small things the beginning of infinite significance, to sense the ultimate in the common and the simple; to feel in the rush of the passing the stillness of the eternal."[6]

The presence of wonder in a healthcare facility is expressed in the way one touches another with reverence, in the transporter's care when he moves a patient, in the way one listens to someone in pain, in the discussions of cases, in the tone of business meetings. It is present when we are reminded that what we do has infinite significance. It is especially evident when the healthcare community is invited to prayer. "To pray is to take notice of the wonder, to regain a sense of the mystery that animates all beings, the divine margin in all attainments."[7]

HUMILITY

Wonder necessarily places all our own achievements within a different perspective. Wonder humbles us. Catholic healthcare in the United States is a vast network of people and institutions, hundreds of facilities and thousands of people. It serves hundreds of thousands of people each year with skill and with amazing technological resources. Its resources are vast, its accomplishments rightly a source of pride. However, Catholic healthcare exists because of the call and the grace of God; its resources belong to the Creator. We heal because God heals; we have skills because God has created us with wonderful capacities for learning and inventing. No one, no group, "owns" Catholic healthcare. We are stewards who cherish the Master's treasure, including the treasure of human life.

Humility is not subservience; it is not the denial of our gifts and talents.

Humility is, above all else, truthfulness. It is recognition of what we have been given and joyful celebration of our dependence on the Giver. Humility joins us with the one who "humbled himself and became obedient unto death, even death on a cross" (Phil 2:8). This humility is expressed in service. It is continuation of the work of the one who did not come to be served but to serve (Mt 20:28).

Catholic healthcare exists to serve people. The physician, the nurse, the sponsor, the administrator, the technician, the finance officer, the board member—all are servants. They do not seek the places of honor at the table (see Lk 14:7-11), but rather join with the one who washes the guests' feet. Genuine service seeks the other's good and places the other first. It values the other and strives to enhance the other's life. Such service is creative and intuitive. It devises ways to serve, imagines new methods, and finds new cures. It also knows when and where service is needed; it does not wait for its neighbors' shouts to recognize a need.

Humility and service express themselves in Catholic healthcare when people recognize their gifts and skills and remember why they have them. Confidence is vital to healthcare; arrogance has no place in it. The most important people in any facility are the ones who are served. Humble healthcare givers do not expect to be called heroes. They reach out to others because they recognize the "obligations of being alive and connected to one another." They work together for the sake of others and value each other in their service. A humble healthcare institution is sensitive to its neighborhood and its people. It does not strive to be the biggest or most important, but to be of the best possible service. It works with other institutions to provide the best possible care for the people. It remembers the reason for its existence and who ultimately directs and enables the work. It takes to heart the first homily of a newly ordained bishop. He recalled how restaurant personnel frequently introduce themselves and say, "I'll be serving you this evening." "Well," said the bishop, "I'm Kenneth, and I'll be serving you for a long, long time."[8]

PERSEVERANCE

"Live by the Word and keep walking." Our survey of the theological foundations of Catholic healthcare has taught us that we need to keep walking; we need to serve for a long, long time. It has also taught us that our God is a persevering companion. The revelation that is the Judaic-Christian tradition tells us that God is one who accompanies. God did not abandon Moses and the people in their infidelity. Jesus promised that he is with us always. The grace of God goes with us in suffering and into death. Believers know they are never alone. There is never a moment when they are abandoned by the saving God. This reality enables us to persevere in a journey that is often difficult and painful.

Healthcare is about suffering and death. It is often about people who suffer for a long, long time, whose deaths seem slow in coming. To continue in compassion and remain attentive to such people is a constant challenge. We are tempted to close our eyes and our ears. Perseverance calls us to enduring sensitivity, to clear vision.

Clear vision is a necessity for the healthcare giver. It is also vital for the healthcare community. The complexities of healthcare today, the demands and pressures facing all healthcare facilities, tempt us to turn away, to give up. We sometimes echo the Exodus people, who wanted to go back to Egypt because it was at least familiar. As with them, we murmur against the changes rather than straining toward the future. We grit our teeth and hang on. At such times, we should recall a Moses who refused to turn back to Egypt, who would not give up on people who were most uncooperative. We need to remember Jesus who would not be dissuaded from going to Jerusalem, even though death awaited him there.

Perseverance is more than grim endurance. Gospel perseverance is filled with hope and confidence. It looks to a future that we do not yet see, even as it recognizes the grace of the moment. To persevere is to abide in the One who abides in us. Perseverance is a faith-filled activity. It is realistic yet not pessimistic. It is hard working yet not frantic. It attends to, but is not overwhelmed by, the signs and questions of the times.

Perseverance expresses itself in the continuing care we give those who suffer, in our constant striving to alleviate suffering and make healthcare more humane. It is also evident in the inspiring constancy of healthcare leaders who struggle to bring Catholic healthcare into the twenty-first century. These are the ones who can say with the author of Hebrews, "But we are not of those who shrink back and are destroyed, but of those who have faith and keep their souls" (Heb 10:39).

Wonder enables perseverance; humility sustains it. Wonder teaches us to sense divine presence in life; humility reminds us who sustains us in the journey. A spirituality for Catholic healthcare needs all three. The experience of healthcare prompts all three.

To serve in healthcare, therefore, is to enter on a journey, to keep walking even in the midst of uncertainty and anguish. Such service can only be sustained in the company of the saints, the men and women who journey with us. The reason for the journey is the needs of our brothers and sisters; its impetus, the call and grace of God. Many today question the future of Catholic healthcare; some doubt it will survive. It will. As long as there are those who are in need *and* those who respond in faith to that need, Catholic healthcare will continue. God's mercy will not be denied. It is ours to heed that mercy, to give it form and substance, and to rejoice in it. It is ours to "live by the Word and keep walking."

Notes

1. Alice Walker, *Living by the Word: Selected Writings 1973-1987,* Harcourt Brace Jovanovich, San Diego, 1988, pp. 1-2.
2. Richard A. McCormick, *Health and Medicine in the Catholic Tradition: Tradition in Transition,* Crossroad Publishing Co., New York, 1985, p. 42.
3. *The Poor Shall Teach Us: A Reflective Process on the Spirituality of Serving with the Poor,* Catholic Health Association, St. Louis, 1990, p. 18.
4. Dennis P. McCann, "'Am I Still My Brother's Keeper?' Theological Reflections on the Crisis in Health Care Management," *Second Opinion,* vol. 8, 1988, p. 86.
5. Walter Burghardt wrote eloquently of Heschel's sense of wonder in "The Health Apostolate: Service, Understanding, Wonder," *Hospital Progress,* February 1983, pp. 30-36.
6. Abraham Joshua Heschel, *The Wisdom of Heschel,* selected by Ruth Marcus Goodhill, Farrar, Straus, and Giroux, New York, 1972, p. 135.
7. Abraham Joshua Heschel, *Quest for God: Studies in Prayer and Symbolism,* Crossroad Publishing Co., New York, 1982, p. 5.
8. Bishop Kenneth Untener made this statement in his homily during the Eucharistic liturgy celebrating his ordination as bishop of the Diocese of Saginaw, MI.

APPENDIX

QUESTIONS FOR REFLECTION AND DISCUSSION

Whatever we read always gains in meaning when we think about it in terms of our own lives and when we talk about it with others. Sometimes it is helpful to have some suggestions to guide our reflection, to start the discussion. The following questions draw out salient points from each chapter of *Food for the Journey.* Hopefully, they will be of assistance in beginning what must be an ongoing reflection.

CHAPTER 1:   *"Take Off Your Shoes, This Is Holy Ground"*

1. Moses would not continue his journey without the presence of God. What is absolutely essential in your journey? What is there, that if taken away, would make you unable or unwilling to continue?
2. People wanted to be near to Jesus because they found life and healing in him. Whom do you like to be near? What do you find in these persons?
3. The presence of God in human experience is always a call to conversion. Do you experience that call in terms of the prodigal son or his older brother? How is that call expressed in terms of your institution?
4. Community happens when God acts to save. Do you feel that the people in your facility work *together?* If so, how and where do you see this? If not, what can you do about it?
5. The presence of God in our lives enables us to hope. What do you hope for? Whom do you hope in? On what do you base your hope?

CHAPTER 2:   *"And They All Were Astonished"*

1. Jesus' healing activity was a concrete expression of his mission. What is your mission? How is it expressed? What is the mission of your institution, and how is it expressed?

2. The gospels tell us that God's kingdom appears in unexpected places and is welcomed by unexpected people. Can you recall an event when you encountered grace/blessing/wisdom in unexpected places or people? What happened, how did you respond?
3. Jesus often healed people by touching them. He frequently touched the "untouchables." Who are the untouchables in your world? How often do you touch them?
4. Jesus listened when others would not. Who is shouting in your life? How often do you take the time to listen to them? What are they saying?
5. When Jesus healed, relationships were restored. How important are relationships in your care of the sick? When have you been instrumental in restoring them, in helping people to rejoin the community?

CHAPTER 3: *"Everybody Needs a Home"*

1. Our homes are expressions of who we are. Where is home for you in the Catholic healthcare ministry? How would you describe it?
2. Church is a home where we discover our identity, are nourished and sent forth to serve. Is this statement true of your experience of Church? How does your facility relate to the local Catholic Church?
3. One of the Church's roles is to provide inspiration. Where do you find inspiration in healthcare today? How would you describe that inspiration?
4. It is important that the Catholic healthcare ministry receive positive recognition by the Catholic Church. Do you feel that such recognition is part of your experience? How?
5. Tradition is vital to the establishment of identity. What are some important traditions in your life, and in the life of your healthcare institution?

CHAPTER 4: *"What Do I Do With All of This Suffering"*

1. Suffering evokes strong responses in all of us. What is your personal response to suffering? Which response (denial, resistance, acceptance) prevails in your facility?
2. All human beings are created in God's image. What does it mean to you that you bear the image of God? How do you recognize God's image in others?

3. The pathos of God accompanies us in our suffering. Can you name a time when you experienced genuine compassion? What happened to you as a result of that experience?
4. Covenant with God means we are responsible for each other. For whom do you feel responsible? To whom do you feel you belong? How is covenant present in your experience of Catholic healthcare?
5. Lamentation gives voice to our grief. What do you need to lament? How do you respond to the cries of others?

CHAPTER 5: *"Will Everything Be Okay?"*

1. "Everyone needs a good theology of death." What is your "theology of death?" How does your healthcare community manifest its response to death?
2. Jesus' death tells us that we are not alone. Who is company for you? Do you ever sense the presence of God in your encounters with death?
3. Jesus' resurrection gives us hope in the face of death. Do you ever see signs that life is ultimately victorious? What challenges your hope?
4. Hope gives us courage. What gives you courage to continue in your ministry? Where is courage needed in Catholic healthcare today?

CHAPTER 6: *"There's Something About the Gospel . . ."*

1. Healthcare does not take place in isolation from the community. What is your neighborhood like? How attuned are you to its day-to-day life, to its needs?
2. For the past hundred years, the Church has consistently addressed the socioeconomic realities of the world. How does this affect your work? What questions does it pose for you?
3. For the Judaic-Christian tradition, justice always implies justice in community. What are your communities? Do they work together for the sake of the common good?
4. Preferential option for the poor demands that we listen to their voices. To whom do you listen on a typical day? Whose voices do you not hear?
5. Justice means truly seeing what is before us. What do you see every day? What do you avoid looking at? What still remains unseen?

CHAPTER 7: *"The Earth Is Breathing Again"*

1. Creation is God's gift to us. It implies our participation in the on-going work of creation. How conscious are you of the gifts that are given to you? Is this consciousness part of deliberations within your institution?
2. One of the resources that we steward is the tradition of the Catholic healthcare ministry itself. What in that tradition gives you cause for hope? What is valuable to you and to those with whom you work?
3. The tradition of the Catholic healthcare ministry is specified in the lives and traditions of individual sponsoring congregations. How often do you celebrate these traditions? How well are they known in your institution?
4. Jesus' parables remind us that stewardship does not mean ownership; it is not domination of resources, material or human. When have you felt challenged to "let go" of control, to be open to new understandings, new experiences? How did you respond?
5. Jesus' parables also tell us that stewardship must be open to risk. What are the greatest risks facing you at the present time? What are the risks facing your facility or your system?

CHAPTER 8: *"It's More Complicated Than That"*

1. Moral character, who we say we are, is influenced by the communities in which we live. What communities have had a formative influence in your life? Which ones are most significant for you now? What do they ask of you?
2. Moral character is expressed in our actions. Can you name a recent event in which your actions expressed your moral commitment? Has a recent corporate action expressed the moral commitment of your institution?
3. Within the Judaic-Christian tradition, moral vision implies both community and covenant. When making decisions, do the leaders you work with ask how this decision will affect you *as a people?* How are integrity and consistency manifested in your activity?
4. Moral vision includes vision of the future. What is your vision, your hope for the future of Catholic healthcare? What is your vision for your own future in Catholic healthcare?
5. Worship shapes and fashions a people. Does your facility provide opportunities for communal worship? Are they meaningful? How do they influence your work together?

EPILOGUE: *"Live by the Word and Keep Walking"*

1. Wonder puts us in touch with the mystery in life. What or who provokes wonder in your life? Is there an element of awe in your experience of the Catholic healthcare ministry?
2. Humility is honest recognition of gifts. What are your gifts? How do you use them in service of others?
3. Perseverance enables us to continue the journey even in difficult times. What keeps you going? What would help you to continue the journey?

The Catholic Health Association of the United States is the national leadership organization of more than 1,200 Catholic healthcare sponsors, systems, facilities, and related organizations and services. Founded in 1915, CHA enables its members to accomplish collectively what they could not achieve individually. The association participates in the life of the Church by advancing the healthcare ministry and by asserting leadership within the Church and the rest of society through programs of advocacy, facilitation, and education.

This document represents one more CHA service. National headquarters: 4455 Woodson Road, St. Louis, MO 63134-3797; 314-427-2500. Washington office: 1776 K Street, NW, Suite 204, Washington, DC 20006-2304; 202-296-3993.